MW01687412

Dr. Olu Oluwa-Tofehinti has authored a brilliant overview of how to build and maintain a healthy marriage. These are clear and helpful keys to counter the stress, strain, and sinister traps set to undermine God's plan for healthy marriages built on trusting and tested relationships. Well done, Dr. Oluwa-Tofehinti.

—Dr. Glen Burris Jnr.,
former President of the Foursquare Church

SECRETS YOUR Counselor WON'T TELL YOU

Keys to Success in Marriage

Dr. Olu Oluwa-Tofehinti

Secrets Your Counselor Won't Tell You

Trilogy Christian Publishers
A Wholly Owned Subsidiary of Trinity Broadcasting Network
2442 Michelle Drive
Tustin, CA 92780

For information about special discounts for bulk purchases, please contact Trilogy Christian Publishing.

Manufactured in the United States of America

10 9 8 7 6 5 4 3 2 1
Library of Congress Cataloging-in-Publication Data is available.

ISBN 978-1-63769-048-2
ISBN 978-1-63769-049-9 (ebook)

DISCLAIMER

Every effort has been made to make this book as complete and accurate as possible. Although the author and publisher have prepared this book with the greatest of care, and have made every effort to ensure the accuracy, we assume no responsibility or liability for errors, inaccuracies, or omissions.

Every effort has been made to make this book as complete and accurate as possible. However, there may be mistakes in typography or content. Also, this book contains information that may help to bring success in marital life. Therefore, this book should be used as a guide, not as the ultimate source of success; Jesus is the ultimate success.

The purpose of this book is to educate. The author and publisher do not warrant that the information contained in this book is fully complete and shall not be responsible for any errors or omissions. The author and publisher shall have neither liability nor responsibility to any person or entity with respect to any loss or damage caused or alleged to be caused directly or indirectly by this book.

ACKNOWLEDGEMENTS

To Jesus, who loved me,
who instituted marriage, intended for it to succeed,
and laid out all guidelines for marriage to work and succeed.

To my beautiful wife Bola
and lovely children Toni, Semi, and Toluwani:
thank you for helping me throughout the process of writing this book.
May the Lord keep on blessing you all forever and always.

WHAT TO EXPECT FROM THIS BOOK?

The best way to utilize this book is to:

1. Read it at least twice
2. Take notes
3. Picture what you want from the book
4. Be willing to pay the price
5. Take responsibility
6. Ask questions
7. Be open to feedback
8. Take actions
9. Embrace change

CONTENTS

The reality of getting married, it really changed things into something beautiful. There was transformation.

—Peter Scolari

Read Verses

Josh. 24:15, Eph. 5:33, 6:1–2, Gen. 2:18–25

INTRODUCTION

My intention in writing this book on marriage is to specifically say that God's plan for marriage from the onset has been one man with one woman for a lifetime. God specifically states that he hates divorce in Malachi 2. But today we find that more than 50 percent of marriages fail. Why?

Do you know that according to a study released by Barna Research Group, Christians are more likely to experience divorce as compared to non-Christians? They found that among born-again Christians, 27 percent are currently divorcing or have previously divorced compared to 24 percent among unbelievers.

Why is this so? You have to recognize that our adversary, the devil, knows the impact we will have if our marriages stay intact, hence why the attack is more on born-again Christians than unbelievers. This has become a culture that has removed the stigma of divorce.

It's my estimation that about one million American children suffer from the divorce of their parents every year. Are you aware that a warfare is ongoing against Christian homes and this battle must be won by the help of God for the sake of this generation and the next?

I had a firsthand experience of this attack even in my marriage. So, writing this book is not for me from what I read but what I have experienced. I believe strongly that what I have to share here will help many marriages. I was devastated because my marriage was about to end while I was busy with life. I was not self-aware of how my behaviors were hurting the person I love most. I was in complete shock and devastated trying to process what I was experiencing.

My marriage is about to end, I told myself. It was that night, alone, that I decided to change my ways and not allow the devil to win this battle. I started asking myself, *how did I get here, to a point where my wife was willing to call it quit?* I got here because of insensitivity, because selfishness, because I was not self-aware, because of busyness, because I had put my ministry before my marriage. *Can you believe it, as a pastor, I help people find success and happiness in life and here am I struggling with mine*, I told myself? Maybe you can relate to this. If yes, you are in the right place.

So, the purpose of this book is to help marriages like mine as much as possible to win this battle against their homes.

What Can Be Done to Promote Success in Marriage and Avoid Divorce?

This is a question that many have struggled to answer. Many have suggested certain solutions, that is: living together without being married, open marriages, no childbearing, communal marriages, or no marriage, at all. So, what are God's answers to these questions?

These are some of the questions that I have looked at in this book. My prayer and hope are that it will help some in their relationships by doing it in God's way and stay married. The book is guided and based on the word of God and on personal experiences.

Some believe that their marriage is healthy and good; but can you make it better or great, which is the essence of this book.

From my personal experience in marriage, I have discovered that many marriages need transformation. Over the course of my practice and research I have found some secrets that could help in this transformational process.

Self-Examination

- At the end of this book, you will know the foundation and the purpose of marriage according to God's mind.
- At the end of this book, you will understand and acknowledge the truth that Jesus Christ is the Son of God even as he is God.
- At the end of this book, you will know that God is not merely an observer of people's marriage but also a marriage participant. He has a marriage of His own.

- At the end of this book, you will know that God's marriage should be the standard of evaluation for all the marriages between men and women. It is the prototype that should be learned from.
- At the end of this book, you will know the basic and significant roles performed by God in His own marriage.
- At the end of this book, you must be willing to be one of the members of the church of God because of the numerous benefits that are jointly attached to them.
- At the end of this book, you will understand the significance of the parable of the Wedding Feast (Matt. 22:1–14).
- At the end of this book, will understand the peril of not receiving the right message invitation into the wedding ceremony.
- At the end of this book, you will be able to distinguish between the wrong message, the incomplete message, and the complete true gospel of Christ.
- At the end of this book, you will believe in the death and the resurrection of Jesus Christ (That is, if you have not believed before).
- Finally, at the end of this book, you must be committed to expressing all the truth that you have acquired in Christ' roles in His own marriage.

MARRIAGE AS REVEALED BY GOD

Marriage is not only a human thing. It is an institution recognized and authorized by God. This may seem too much to comprehend at this point. However, this section of this book is committed to bringing you into these realities. In this section, it will be shown that the foundation of marriage is God, and the purpose of marriage is to reveal the love of God. For perfect understanding, this section will premise its claims on the teaching on the divinity of Jesus Christ. Thus, this section aims to bring you into the full alignment of your will to God's will with respect to marriage.

The Prototype of All Genuine Marriages

The first time the Scripture said anything about marriage was in Genesis.

Genesis 2: 24 says: "Therefore a man shall leave His father and mother and be joined to His wife and they shall become one flesh."

With the term "Therefore," it is clear that this verse is a conclusion. It is a truth to which all the exercise of making a woman out of a man is geared towards. This is the verse that instituted the idea of marriage as depicted in the oneness or inseparability of two distinct entities.

Now, it is time we take a closer look at the verse. There is something funny about this verse that people don't usually recognize. This is after the creation of the first man and the first woman. There was nothing like father and mother because there were no children or people other than Adam and Eve. Yet here is this verse' it's talking about a man leaving His father and mother. For this reason, it makes more sense when these words are more understood prophetically than they are understood literally.

Paul in His writings to the people of Ephesus understood this method of Bible study very well, and he indeed gave a new insight towards the concept of marriage using this method. Ephesians 5:31–32 says: "For this reason a man shall leave his father and mother and be joined to his wife, and the two shall become one flesh.. This is a great mystery, but I speak concerning Christ and the church."

This is great! The writer of Ephesians has helped us through the tedious processes of searching the purpose and meaning of the Genesis 2:24 prophecy. With this, we understand the true meaning of this scripture. The first time the Scriptures spoke about marriage, the Scripture spoke about the marriage of God (Christ) and the church. If we refer to the previous pages, it has already been affirmed that Jesus Christ is God, but we are yet to know who the church is.

Jesus Christ Is God

The book of John is notable for being loud on the fact that Jesus Christ is God. To show the importance of this truth to the whole world, the book expresses it in its opening verse. Speaking concerning Jesus Christ, John 1:1 states, "In the beginning was the Word, and the Word was with God, and the Word was God."

"The Word" as contained here is metaphoric to the person of Jesus Christ. Therefore, it can be interchanged for the name Jesus Christ.

To buttress this point, the writer of Hebrews also expresses that same truth. The writer of Hebrews calls Jesus the express image of the person of God (Heb. 1:3). In clearer terms, the eighth verse of this same chapter states, "But unto the Son he says, Thy throne, o God, is forever and ever" (Heb. 1:8).

The knowledge that "Jesus is God" is very integral to this section of the book. This is because it is the foundation for the truth that God is not merely an observer of marriage but a participant himself. If God is a participant of marriage, then there is a great lesson that we can learn from how he plays His role in marriage.

Having understood that the foundation of marriage as contained in the beginning of the marriage of God and a body of Christ (the church), we can derive all understanding of what a marriage should be from this prototype. Here, we will be looking at God's role in His own marriage.

God's Role in His Own Marriage

Forgiveness and Forgetfulness of Sins

God not only forgives the sins of His partner (that is the body of believers) but also, He promised to remember the sins no more. Jeremiah 31:34 states:

> No more shall every man teach his neighbor, and every man his brother, saying, 'Know the LORD,' for they all shall know Me, from the least of them to the greatest of them, says the LORD. For I will forgive their iniquity, and their sin I will remember no more.

The first thing he did in this verse that reveals His role in His marriage was to make Himself known to His partner. As a spouse who is committed to doing the will of God, it is essential that you make yourself known to your partner. You don't have to hide anything from your partner. Also, you must be willing to express the loving aspect of your personality. This loving aspect comprises forgiveness of all the sins of your partner. Just like God, you should not only forgive, but you should also remember the wrongs that your partner does no more. Forgiveness of sins is very important in marriage. Certainly, there will be sins against one another. In all of this, you should always remember the lesson you have learnt from the original marriage which is forgiveness and oblivion of sins.

Channel of Blessings

Ephesians 1:3 says, "Blessed be the God and Father of our Lord Jesus Christ, who has blessed us with all spiritual blessings in heavenly places in Christ." This is a great virtue that we can emulate from Christ in His marriage. He made Himself become a channel of blessings to His church. Some of us in our relationship may have better opportunities than our partners. In this case, you have to see yourself as a platform to channel all the blessings to your spouse also. That one of the partners is constrained should not be a problem since the other partner is in high position; he or she can receive the blessings and channel it to the other. Another thing we can learn from this marriage is that the blessings of one is the blessing of the other. This is because they are interconnected. As it is understood, God blessed the church in Christ. In this sense, the blessing of God could locate the church in Him. Also, partners must have quality thoughts of each other evident in each other's hearts. God recognizes this level of intimacy and through this, He can use one as a point of contact to express blessings to the other. The husband and the wife must be interconnected and channel all blessings as received from God and as encountered in the world to each other.

Eternal Fellowship

Jesus Christ promised His church His eternal presence and fellowship. He would not divorce His church for any reason whatsoever. In Matthew 28:20b, He said, "I am with you always, even unto the end of the age." There is nothing more certain in all the roles of Jesus Christ to His church than His eternal presence in His Church. He sets no time nor space limit to this eternal fellowship. It is certain that He would continually honor His sacred vows with His spouse.

In this light, there should be an assurance of fellowship and commitment in our marriage. Do not threaten your partner with a divorce but instead always express your undying commitment to always be with them through the thick and thin of life. To fulfill His vows to a great extent, He lives within His church. The rhetorical question of 1 Corinthians 2:16 which states, "Know ye not that ye are the temple of God, that the Spirit of God dwells in you?" affirms the habitability of Christ within His church. A partner also must in the same fashion allow his or her reality to find existence in his/her spouse. Fellowship is an integral part of every marriage as it is expressly contained in the prototype of all marriages as established by God Himself. In cases where the partners are working in different locations, do not let space and time give cessation to the existence of your partner in your heart. Hold your fellowship with your partner above all things.

Unconditional Love

One of the primary virtues that is found in the marriage of Christ and the church is a love that is without condition. Paul said:

> For I am persuaded, that neither death, nor life, nor angels, nor principalities, nor powers, nor things present, nor things to come, nor height, nor depth, nor any other created thing, shall be able to separate us from the love of God, which is in Christ Jesus our Lord.
>
> —Romans 8:38–39

What exactly do you think gave Paul that guarantee that the love that binds Christ and the Church was not a kind of love that could be broken? He must have learnt of the nature of the love of God. The unconditional nature of the love of God is expressly contained in the Psalm 89:30–34. It states:

If His sons forsake my law and do not walk in my judgments: if they break my statutes and do not keep my commandments: Then I will punish their transgression with the rod and their iniquity with stripes. Nevertheless, my loving-kindness I will not utterly take from him, nor allow my faithfulness to fail. My covenant I will not break, nor alter the word that is gone out of my lips.

This is the nature of the love of God. Christ has a moral standard, and every individual has the same. In this section, we can see the unconditional love of God; as He says even if His moral standards are defied by His human partners, He will use His rod, yet He will not stop loving. The rod and the stripes are not literal. They symbolize correction.

What Christ is saying here is that the defiance of His church will not make him break His covenant of everlasting love. Also, any correction that will be expressed on the defiance will be done in love. Also, we all have our own do's and don'ts in a marriage or any relationship. If your partner defies your do's and don'ts (this will surely happen), you are required to maintain your steadfast love as Christ's. Also, you are to correct in love and not harshly, since correction is also very important in love. You see that Christ attaches correction to His love. However, "stripes and rods" as used in the scriptural passage are not literal expressions, but they are figurative to the term "correction and teaching." Not even a moral offense of any sort should break our marital vows of love. This is manifested in the prototype of all genuine marriages which is the marriage of Christ and the church.

Everlasting Marriage

There is nothing more emphatic in the word of God than His everlasting marriage to the church. This teaches us emphatically that marriage ought not to be given to divorce at all. It is lack of knowledge of the will of God for every situation that makes people break marriages.

Once again, in the prophetic words of Hosea, the nature of the marriage of Christ to His church is found. Hosea 2:17 says, "In that day," declares the Lord, you will call me 'my husband'; you will no longer call me 'my master.'" Here, it can be seen that God understands that He plays a leadership and an all-powerful role in this marriage, yet He does not want to keep His partner in awe of Him. It is clear that He wants to be seen more as a marital partner than as a master. He wanted love to be the driving instinct of the relationship and not merely the fear of being punished by a supreme and sovereign God. This is a very salient point to the men in marriage. It is true that God has given you the leadership position. However, there are times you can give silence to the authority and come down to a level of intimacy to your spouse.

Going further, He made a very sacral pledge in the Hosea 2:19–21. What does the marriage of Christ to His church really characterize? Verses 19-20 is loud on the features of this marriage as it expressly states, "I will betroth you to me forever: yes, I will betroth you to me in righteousness and justice, in lovingkindness and mercy. I will betroth you to me in faithfulness, and you shall know the Lord."

What a husband is the Lord Jesus Christ. He promised a marriage that will not only be forever but will also characterize His righteousness, His faithfulness, His love, His compassion, and His justice. He promised all this to His church without compromise. With a righteous, loving, compassionate, and faithful partner; it is obvious that Christ is prepared to glue the oneness of His marriage forever.

In the same way, imitate the prototype of all marriages. Let your own marriage be graced with your love and compassion. Surely, that partner of yours will offend you greatly, but with a righteous, loving, faithful, and compassionate heart, you can always uphold your marriage forever.

Application: Imitate the prototype of God's marriage. Let your own marriage be graced with your love and compassion. Surely, that partner of yours will offend you greatly, but with a righteous, loving, faithful, and compassionate heart, you can always uphold your marriage forever. Specifically, husbands, follow the example of God's leadership. Be more a marital partner than a master. Let love, not fear drive your marriage.

Sameness of Body

When Genesis says the two shall be one body, it was indeed referring to the marriage of Christ and the church. It has been found that many people say these things on their wedding days, but they do not really have a correct understanding of it. It is the principle of same identity. Christ made Himself have the same identity with His church. In 1 Corinthians 12:27, the church is stated to be Christ's own very body: "Now, you are the body of Christ and members in individually." In the same way that you give nourishment and respect to your body, you have to give nourishment and respect to the body of your partner because you are the same body.

The idea that the church is the same body with Jesus Christ may be kind of complex. However, we can take a closer look into the operation of this actuality. When the writer of Ephesians spoke of the blessing of God he stated, "Blessed be the God and Father of our Lord Jesus Christ, who hath blessed us with all spiritual blessings in heavenly places in Christ." We can see that the church is in Christ. He puts the church within Himself. With this, the identity of one cannot be seen outside the other. Also, His residence in His church synthesizes the two identities into one.

Speaking of the mystery, Paul stated in Colossians 1:27, "To them God willed to make known what are the riches of the glory of this mystery among the Gentiles: which is Christ in you, the hope of glory." Christ lives in His church which comprises of all people who believe in His words. We can apply this thought system to our marriage. Let your spouse be richly contained in your heart to the extent that you cannot see yourself without seeing your spouse within you. This is the bedrock of all Christ-like marriage.

Ponder on this note of Ephesians and commit yourself to living out the words. "So, husbands ought to love their own wives as their own bodies. He that loves his wife loves himself" (Eph. 5:28).

Offering of the Word

Word is a creative force. Without the word of God, the world would not have been created. Because of this, the offering of words is an integral part of a good marriage. It is the creative force of one. All that has been shown thus far has been centered on God's word to His church. As it has been seen, these words characterize the hopes and the truth upon which their relationship is built.

Just as Christ has furnished the church with His words, the church also reiterates these words to Christ through prayers and songs. The same should be adopted in our marital homes. Let the words of the husband be seasoned with grace to the wife, and let the wife at all times honor the husband with the words of her mouth. It is by words that you can shape your partner into the perfect picture you want them to be.

Ephesians 5:25–26 clears it all when Paul states, "Husbands, love your wives, even as Christ also loved the church, and gave himself for it: That he might sanctify her, having cleansed her with the washing of water with the word." In this verse, we see that the Bible likened the words of Christ to water by which He cleanses the church. For a prosperous marriage, you should also adopt the method of using the word of God to wash yourselves from the filth of this world. In conclusion, the words spoken into marriage by its participants are the defining characteristics of that marriage. Let your words to your marriage be derived from Christ's words to His marriage.

Perfect Perception

Do you know that mental perception is more powerful than physical perception? We see people the way we perceive them in our mind. That is the reason why when a person you have known to be wicked does something good; you still can't see any changes in the person. Here, we will be considering how God perceives the church whom He is in an everlasting marriage with. Psalm 16:3 says the goodness of Christ extends to the saints that are in the earth, and to the excellent, in whom is all His delight. He sees His saints as excellent and He is absolutely delighted in them. This same way, you are to adopt a right mental perception of seeing your spouse as excellent, and you should treat your mind not to find faults in him or her but to be delighted in him or her.

With this kind of mental perception, the marriage will grow in love and in corrections made out of love. The content of Christ's mental perception of the church is evident in our anchor scripture. Ephesians 5:25–27 states:

> Husbands, love your wives, even as Christ also loved the church, and gave himself for it: That he might sanctify her, having cleansed her with the washing of water with the word. that He might present her to Himself a glorious church, not having spot or wrinkle or any such thing, but that she should be holy and without blemish.

Here, we see Jesus presenting His church to Himself as glorious, spotless, and without faults. Since we human beings are the church, we both know we have faults. However, in spite of all our imperfect nature, Christ sees spotlessness, holiness, and perfection in us. This is indeed a virtue that we can emulate in our marriage. We should learn to always see the good sides of our partners and to always nourish this goodness with the words of our mouth.

Submission and Honor

We have mostly seen the good sides of Jesus Christ. It is time we learnt from the role of the church also in this marriage. The church submits to the authority and lordship of Jesus Christ. This is evident in many texts of the epistles. Ephesians 5:21–22 states: "Submitting to one another in the fear of God. Wives submit to your own husbands as to the Lord." As a wife, you have a role to submit yourself to the authority of your husband. Many people have always quoted this verse that teaches all wives to submit themselves to the authority of their husbands as though they are submitting themselves to the Lord.

Quoting this, the attention of submission is always diverted to the wives only. Let us take a look at the prior verse. It states, "Submitting yourselves one to another in the fear of the Lord." This is clear. It implies that it is not only the wives that should emulate the virtue of submission, but the two partners should recognize and submit to the authority of each other respectively. In a marriage where this is done, with less emphasis on the patriarchal role of the man, there would be a lasting success. With this, the man knows he has a duty to honor the moral standards of His wife even as the wife honors His own laws and commandments in the marriage. A marriage where submission is one-sided with the wife only submitting to the husband is yet to attain its full potential. Conclusively, the two partners must submit to each other.

Intercession

Intercession simply means standing in the place of prayer on behalf of another person. This is one of the necessities that every partner in a marriage must perform. You are to constantly intercede for your spouse when you pray. Prayer is a virtue that is essential to all believers in Christ. It is only prayers that can save people from the terrors and dangers of this world. The Scripture showed Jesus Christ praying for His church at many instances. For reference, you can see John 17. Also, He ever lives to intercede for His church. Hebrews 7:25 states, "Therefore he is able to save to the uttermost those who come to God through him, since He always lives to make intercession for them." Yes, this is one of the roles of Christ in His marriage. He lives to make intercession for His church.

Jesus' marital life is indeed the epitome of what partners should do in their own marital life. You have to pray not for yourself only but for your partner also. Some partners will say "I used to pray for him or her before, but I just stopped." You cannot let anything affect your prayer for your partner. As a matter of fact, not even their bad deeds should give you reason to stop praying for your partner. Whether your partner is good towards you or bad towards you, you are required to always intercede for them before God. This is your reasonable service.

These are indeed quality insights that have been derived from the marital life of God. We should invest our time into making this teaching become our own reality. There are many more roles that God perform in His marriage. The ten key points shown in this section is just a part of them. However, if we are committed to practicing this in our marriage, it is bound to be successful. There is a guarantee of a perfect result. The marriage of Christ to the church is the original marriage from which all other marriages should be derived. A man that desires a peaceful home must imitate God in His own marriage.

The marriage of Christ is indeed the foundation being the first to be spoken of, and the purpose of all marriage being the focal area of the whole Scripture.

Criterion for Learning from the Marriage of Christ

The clear example of the marriage of Christ is not just a show-off. In a sincere sense, God expects all human beings to learn from the nature of the marriage of His Son. This is not only because it is the oldest marital union; it is also the grand marital union that should be observed by all. The marriage of Christ and His church has remained beautiful, peaceful, perfect, and glorious for millennia now. It remains a truth acknowledged by many children of God and the written word of God that the contract of the marriage is not yet broken and it is still valid up to date.

Without a doubt, it can be clearly seen that if we can adopt the nature of this marriage into our homes, there will be a perennial and permanent peace and fulfillment. However, there is one huge problem. To the believers, it is not a problem at all; to the unbelieving, though, it is a serious problem. Clearly, the marriage of Christ and the church is not just something conditioned by a mere moral principle. It is a marriage founded upon the genuine will of God.

From a Christian standpoint, it is absolutely futile for you to impose the will of God on a natural and unbelieving man or woman. 1 Corinthians 2:14 says it all. It states: "But the natural man does not receive the things of the Spirit of God, for they are foolishness to him; nor can he know them, because they are spiritually discerned." As it has been seen, this teaching cannot be understood by anyone who is yet to believe in the gospel of Christ. To God, that person yet remains a natural man. This is because it is the belief of Christ that makes a person a spiritual man by the virtue of the Spirit of God residing in the person.

In a way, it is absolutely impossible for an unbeliever to understand the chapter above and to work in that light. The person will just have access to such rich content from a moral point of view and not from an edifying point of view. And if you must know, the single problem of morality is that it is liable to be defied by human beings. Therefore, even if you are committed to following the roles of Jesus Christ as taught above, you will fail if you are not a believer of His Gospel. In Philippians 2:13, the Scripture says, "For it is God who works in you both to will and to do for His good purpose." Yes, it is the duty of God to inspire you to obey His own will. It is not by power and by might but by the Spirit of God. From this, we can understand that unless you are a believer of the word of God, the purpose of your marriage is far from being fulfilled.

It is possible that you are even doing great in your marriage. Your husband is the managing director of a multi-billion-dollar company, and you are already pursuing your second Ph.D. It may even be that your marriage is absolutely problem-free from your own perspective. However, clearly your marriage is not in line with the purpose and the will of God if you are not in Christ. For it to be in line with the purpose and the will of God, it has to be founded on Jesus Christ.

As it has been clearly seen, it takes more than just human will for a marriage to adhere to Jesus Christ. It takes the intervention of God himself. If you are yet to have an intervention of God in your life. If you are yet to have an encounter with the saving grace of God, then the subsequent section is specifically written for you. It is a call for you to be among the church who enjoy the benefit of the lordship and marital partnership of Jesus Christ.

The next section is the most important and core part of this book. It is your belief in this gospel that makes you fulfill God's purpose for marriage. If you are already a believer of the gospel, I celebrate you greatly. However, you can also give your attention to the next section; you sure have something to learn.

THE GOSPEL OF JESUS: THE PROPOSAL FOR ETERNAL MARRIAGE

There are many misconceptions about what the Gospel of Jesus Christ is. Sadly, this means that not all who belong to the church are indeed members of the church of God. Going to church does not make you a follower of Christ.

How to Start a Relationship with God

Like many people, I didn't grow up as a believer, I was religious, I attend church, but my understanding of having a relationship with God was next to zero. As you read these few pages, I would like to share with you not my opinion but what God says in His word, the Bible. The Bible is very clear: God loves you, and He cares about you regardless of your failures, hurts, and struggles etc.

Here's what He has for you: irrespective of what you think or how good you are, He says we have all sinned. We fall short of the glory of God. Not in the sense that we put our sins on a scale, but that we've missed the mark. As far as God is concerned, to be accepted, we need to be perfect for He is perfect, we need to score 100 percent. If we score less that one hundred in God's eyes, it's a failure. He is perfect, He is pure, He is holy. So, as far as God is concerned, there is no less than 100 percent. We can't just be good enough or religious enough.

So that we understand the perspective of God, the Bible says, "For by grace you have been saved through faith, and that not of yourself; it is the gift of God" (Eph. 2:8). This means you can't work your way into a relationship with God. So, to have a relationship with God, you have to admit that you've offended a holy God. You may think your religiosity, or your morality will make you acceptable to God, but all these are also sins that cause you and me to fall short of the glory of God i.e., our religiosity, our so-called morality, because you cannot be good or religious enough for a Holy God.

In addition, not only have we all sinned, but the wages of sin is death (Rom. 6:23). This means that my sins deserve to be paid the wage of spiritual death, which is separation from God forever. I know some have a head knowledge about this, but you can't just have head knowledge about this. Unless you address your sin, it will keep you separated from God for all eternity. The Bible says God's not willing that any person should perish but that everyone should come to a knowledge of Christ.

Though you can't do anything to merit a relationship with God and though you have sinned, He doesn't want you to perish. Because of this, God sent His son Jesus, fully God, fully man, to die on the cross to pay for and cover your sin. "For God so loved the world that He gave His only begotten son that whoever believes in Him should not perish but have everlasting life" (John 3:16). Everlasting life starts the moment you act on this information, the moment you put your faith in Christ. Though your sins are paid for by His sacrifice on that Calvary cross, and by the blood He shed, you still need to receive Him by faith.

And He says the way you do it is by stepping out in faith to receive Him and acknowledge that sacrifice.

You say, "Lord Jesus, I have sinned against you. I want to ask you to forgive me and I want you to come into my life now. Cleanse me, make me yours." As many as receive Him, the Bible says, He gives the right to become children of God, even to those who believe in His name.

And so, I don't know where you're at, but you just need to receive Him, ask Him to be the Lord of your life. That may seem too easy or too simple, but He says it's a gift. He says, "Unless you open the door of your heart, turn from your sin, ask me to come in, I'll stay on the outside."

And God is saying to you right now in this very moment, "If you will turn to me, if you will say, 'Lord Jesus, I'm sorry, I've missed it, I have sinned, I've offended you, I've even hurt other people that I'm very sorry, will you forgive me, will you cleanse me from all my sin, will you come into my life right now?' I will come in as I have promised." Everyone who calls upon the name of the Lord will be saved. He loves you. He cares for you. He wants you to know in this moment on this very day at this very time that you can have everlasting life.

Now what are you going to do? Will you trust Him and accept Him? Will you turn away? The decision is yours.

If you would like to pray to receive Christ now, you can pray this prayer: "Lord Jesus, I want to ask you to forgive me of my sin. I admit that I have sinned against you, but on this day, I invite you to come into my life to forgive me of my sin. I believe you died for me, you rose from the dead, and I'm asking you to be my savior."

I assure you, if you have just prayed that prayer, He will answer you. Congratulations!

The following verses will help you understand what God says is now true of your relationship with Him. You might think that you chose to believe in Jesus, much like choosing a house or car. But the following shows God's involvement in you becoming a Christian.

> But as many as received Him, to them He gave the right to become children of God, to those who believe in His name.
>
> —John 1:12

> Just as He chose us in Him before the foundation of the world, that we should be holy and without blame before Him in love.
>
> —Eph. 1:4

> But God, who is rich in mercy, because of His great love with which He loved us.
>
> —Eph. 2:4

> He has delivered us from the power of darkness and conveyed us into the kingdom of the Son of His love.
>
> —Col. 1:13

> Much more then, having now been justified by His blood, we shall be saved from wrath through Him.
>
> —Rom. 5:9

> Therefore, if anyone is in Christ, he is a new creation; old things have passed away; behold, all things have become new.
>
> —2 Cor. 5:17

Explaining the Parable of the Wedding Feast (Matt. 22:1–14)

The parable of the wedding feast speaks of a great king who invited people to partake in the blessings of the marriage of His son. It happened that the originally invited guests ignored the invitation of the king to the extent that they even beat up his messengers. Since the original invited guests had ignored the invitation, the king charged his messengers to go to the streets. This time, they were to invite everybody. They were to invite not only the special people but the Toms, Dicks, and Harries also. The messengers did as sent. They invited many guests. However, at the feast, it was found that one of the guests was putting on the wrong clothes. Certainly, he didn't have the invitation letter and as such, didn't know of the dress code. The king was so angry at the man that had entered erroneously that he commanded that the man should be thrown into a place of utmost distress and pain.

So, what do the symbols in the parable mean? The king symbolizes God. The son of the king symbolizes Jesus Christ. The invitation call symbolizes the gospel of Christ. The messengers symbolize the evangelists, prophets and the apostles who preached the gospel of Christ. The people that ignored the invitation symbolizes the unbelievers. The people that honored the invitation symbolizes all believers. Finally, the man that was put in eternal suffering; he is the focal area of this discourse. The man symbolizes those who think they are believers, yet they have never received the gospel of Christ. They didn't have any invitation letter to that eternal and perfect marriage. They thought they were members of the feast, but they were fake. Their presence was not recognized. They came in erroneously. As a matter of fact, their presence annoyed the celebrants. The end of such people is just as precarious as the end of those who never believed.

The True Gospel: The Wedding Invitation

The content of the gospel is clear. It was the reason for what we call "Christianity" today. It is the singular fact that has been emphasized by all the apostles. It is surprising today that some of the so-called messengers of the king are so stingy in sharing the invitation letter to everyone as directed by the king. Some messengers have found pleasure in exchanging the true invitation letter for a fake one. Do not worry. The apostle Paul would not have His audience ignorant of what the true gospel is. He expressly stated in 1 Corinthians 15:1–4:

> Moreover, brethren, I declare to you the gospel which I preached to you, which also you received and in which you stand, by which also you are saved, if you hold fast that word which I preached to you—unless you believed in vain.
>
> For I delivered to you first of all that which I also received: that Christ died for our sins according to the Scriptures, and that He was buried, and that He rose again the third day according to the Scriptures.

This message of Paul's is integral, essential, and tied to all that has been taught on. That is why the apostle said anything; otherwise, this truth is tantamount to a "belief in vain." This is indeed the content of the invitation letter the king sent out. The letter contained the fact that His Son died for the sins of all people and that He was resurrected on the third day. This singular fact is the foundational truth of it all. In 1 Corinthians 15:14, he boldly said, "And if Christ is not risen, then our preaching is empty, and your faith is also empty." If Christ has not been raised, then there would be no wedding feast, and all that was taught in the marriage of Christ would be wrong. However, the truth is that Christ does indeed rise from the dead. Verse 20 of the same chapter said it clearly that Christ was indeed raised from the dead and to this end, he was seen by many more than five hundred people. They were both scriptural and perceptual testimonies that attest to this resurrection. If you have received this invitation as sent by the king in the parable of Jesus (Matt. 22:1–14) then surely you will be welcome in the wedding, not as a mere visitor but as a celebrant.

Following from all that you have learned, you have to believe that Jesus is the Son of God unto His death for the sins of humanity and His resurrection. This is the truth of what the gospel is.

NURTURING THE HEART FOR A PERFECT MARRIAGE

The heart of a person is a substance in marriage that cannot be left untouched. It is a great thing to have laid your marriage upon the foundation of Christ and His church. However, there are more things you should do. For instance, guarding the heart diligently and feeding it with the right word. If your heart is not well furnished, you will just be like the chair in the barber shop, spinning in one spot without making any progress forward. A marriage of those who are involved have not been able to work on their hearts will at best be stagnant and at worse be destructive to the partners.

The book of Proverbs teaches us the importance of the heart. Proverbs 4:20–23 says:

> My son, give attention to my words; Incline your ear to my sayings. Do not let them depart from your eyes; Keep them in the midst of your heart; For they are life to those who find them, And health to all their flesh. Keep your heart with all diligence, for out of it spring the issues of life.

Here, the book of Proverbs shows us the importance of guarding the heart after a good teaching. The writer charged His audience to remember all they have been taught, but he emphasized the need to guard the heart.

According to a submission proposed by Barna Research Group, research shows that Christians are equally likely to experience divorce as non-Christians (Research Releases in Family and Kids—March 31, 2008). This in turn shows that knowledge alone is not sufficient for a good marriage. There is a need for a practical knowledge on some things you should not do. Thank God in the last chapter, you have seen and learnt many things to do from the roles of Christ in His own marriage. Here, you will be taught the things you ought not to do at all.

In this light, we will be highlighting habits that are contaminating to the heart. Hence, they are also destructive to the marriage.

Twelve Dangers to Guard Your Hearts From

1. Active Mentoring to or from the Opposite Sex

People tend to destroy their own marriages by themselves. The motifs that get most marriages destroyed are not commonly the bad ones. I observe that most marriages suffer damage because people tend to do the right things in the wrong ways. A great example of doing the good thing the wrong way is actively having the opposite sex as your mentor or mentoring the opposite sex by yourself.

It is good to have a career mentor. However, if the mentor is of the opposite sex, it is very important you apply wisdom. Your partner may be obviously jealous, and this has a way of ruining homes. In cases where you are so attached to your mentor of the opposite sex, make sure you make the mentoring as passive as it can be. Instead of having closed-door encounters, you can make phone calls, buy books, or even listen to audio or video messages. It can be embarrassing to the points that husbands call some pastors and threaten to kill them if they don't stop having extra marital affair with their wives.

Pastors also have to exhibit wisdom. Instead of having an after-service meeting with an opposite sex member within the confines of your office, you can have the meeting in a more public place. Let the parishioners have a visual encounter of what is going on. However, you can lower your voices for the sake of confidentiality. Also, mentors must ensure their wives or partners are carried along. Let your wife know what you are in for. It will be most disgraceful if a pastor's wife or husband is seen locking themselves up in public with the charge of adultery or another marital unlawfulness. It may even be better if you make it a joint mentoring affair, with your spouses involved.

2. Alien and Ungodly Counsel

This seems funny. Yes, there are indeed some counsels that are alien and ungodly and unless you block your ears from such counsels, they are bound to destroy your home.

It is funny that this kind of counsel is usually given by some people who claim they are from God. They will always tell people what the Lord says. It is good to have words of knowledge about someone. However, it becomes a problem when what the pastor tells you the Lord says contrasts what the Lord says in the Scriptures.

If any pastor tells you the Lord says you should divorce your wife or husband without a valid reason that your life is at risk or adultery has been committed, you must ignore such pastor. This is because divorce is never in the original plan of God (see Matt. 5:31–32). God does not want divorce, and he is not a proponent of divorce.

Let us see Paul's conclusion about those who are married to unbelievers. 1 Corinthians 7:10–13 says,

> Now to the married I command, yet not I but the Lord: A wife is not to depart from her husband. But even if she does depart, let her remain unmarried or be reconciled to her husband. And a husband is not to divorce his wife. But to the rest I, not the Lord, say: If any brother has a wife who does not believe, and she is willing to live with him, let him not divorce her. And a woman who has a husband who does not believe, if he is willing to live with her, let her not divorce him.

As it has been clearly seen, divorce is not of God. Finally, I leave you to ponder and act on Proverbs 14:7 which states: "Go from the presence of a foolish man, when you do not perceive in him the lips of knowledge."

3. Sexual Pleasure with Things

A narrow way to treat the issue of cheating in a marriage is to think it is only when one of the parties come in physical or psychological contact with someone of the opposite sex that cheating is done. This is the most obvious level of cheating. Cheating can happen in different forms. In cases where one of the agents of the marriage has found sexual fulfilment in objects or things and thus denies his or her partner the erotic benefit of marriage, he is cheating. That kind of marriage is highly destructible.

If you want a lasting and promising marriage, you must stop finding sexual fulfilment in mere material things other than your legitimate spouse. If you struggle in this area, as imperative as this is, I know it may not be easy but you should stop. If you continue it may destroy your marriage. For this reason, you should communicate this to your partner (Depending on how reasonable he or she can be), or you can see a trained counselor.

4. Pornography

Pornography is any form of art that is created to arouse sexual feelings in a person. It may not really be a video but written words. It may even come in the form of drawings and sculpture. You have to protect yourself from such.

Pornography introduces a person to different human body structures and statures, different sexual requirements, and different levels of ecstasy.

The problem then is if your partner cannot fulfill these criteria, the pornography audience has the tendency to want to explore other persons. Without doubt, this will result to giving the marriage a deathblow that may never be recovered from.

Flee from pornography. Let us consider a possible question that someone may ask. *What if my husband and I consent to see pornography together that we may learn new things? With the alignment of purpose, can I freely enjoy porn?*

Again, I emphasize. The status of pornography is abetting. It abets adultery and sexual desires with women or men other than your spouse. For example, in the real world, you are approached by someone having the same physique with the porn character whom you find very interesting. The second thought of going down the erotic lane with that person will surely be stirred in your heart. With the images of the pornography in your heart, you are most likely to give in to the person's request.

Conclusively, it is bad for couples to learn new things from pornography. If there is need to learn new things, get books that are thematic to great sexual performance. Avoid visual images of people in that act.

5. Lies

Lying is one of the most disgusting thing that can be in a person's life. Do you know one amazing truth about each lie? It is like a pig. It is very dirty and also prolific. This implies that a lie usually gives birth to many lies.

For a lie to remain standing, it has to be covered up with many more lies. This is indeed why the Bible emphatically calls the devil a liar.

If you have been nurturing a lie or lies in your marriage, then it is time you become bold and speak to your spouse concerning it. I know it is not an easy decision to make, but if you keep going on that lying lane, there is a great furnace at the end of the road. If the truth is too much for you to convey alone, you can look for someone your partner reveres and shares personal information with to accompany you in conveying the truth. There is no foundation as strong and solid as the truth; it is the best foundation to stand on. Truth is very essential in any marriage. Even in Christ's marriage, lies are greatly abhorred. Proverbs 12:22 says, "Lying lips are an abomination to the Lord, But those who deal truthfully are His delight."

Truth is the perfect glue of all godly marriages. It will be unwise if you fail to use this perfect glue in your home. No matter how bad it sounds, always let your partner know what you are going through. And always express true repentance after you have revealed the truth.

I leave you to ponder and act on the words of Paul as contained in Colossians 3:9 that states, "Do not lie to one another, since you have put off the old man with his deeds."

6. Gambling

Although, the Scripture seems to be silent on the discourse of gambling, we cannot shy away from the fact that it has become a salient issue in this age. Gambling is a great distraction that begins in a minor way. This usually applies to the husbands in marriage or relationship. Also, it may apply to some few wives. Many counselors don't usually trace marital detriments to gambling. However, after much inquisition, it is found that a great percentage of men whose marriage didn't work out are gamblers. According to OnlineDivorce Texas, 8 percent of marriages end up in divorce due to this addiction, and these are only counting those couples who indicated the reason for their divorce when filing!

One of the effects of gambling is that it determines the mood of its players. Gambling tells them when they should be happy and when they should be sad. Men who are gamblers usually have mood swings. Today, they come home happy and for the next four days, they come home sad and attitudinal. Even with online gambling today, this is even made worse. All these are passive reactions that gradually and slowly destroy marriages. The worst thing is that the gamblers may not even know his or her marriage is already suffering from their own inconsistencies to pay bills, mood swings, lack of attention to partner, diversion from goals and its accomplishments, and other marital necessities. At the addictive level, gamblers stake everything, including their marriage. You may be thinking, "Is that really possible?"

When a man steals from his wife all because of the uncontrollable urge to gamble, he is already staking his marriage.

If you want a marriage that you can be proud of, you must pick up your mop and clean spots like gambling from your heart.

7. Drinking, Drugs, and Clubbing

A person given to these addictive events and substances is not only destroying himself, but also passively destroying all that he claims to love. Permit my gender insensitivity. It applies to both sexes.

It is very dangerous or detrimental to constantly relate with your spouse under the influence of alcohol. Certainly, being high will make you do and say things you ordinarily would not have said especially if provoked. Your spouse is surely bound to provoke at times, but while being under the influence, you will not be able to manage such occasions well.

The best thing for you is to stop this for the prosperity of your marriage. In cases where there is already an overwhelming desire to do these things, talk to your spouse about it. Remember, no ground is as safe as the truth to stand on.

8. Continual Conversation with Ex-Partners

A careless mistake that some partners make in their marriage is their inability to deal with their ex-partner(s). As a partner, you already told your spouse about your past life.

Some may even go further by disclosing the sensitive details of their past relationship such as erotic escapades and other sensitive things.

It will be a great error to keep being in either physical or technological contact with that partner. Some may even be found in a restaurant with an ex. Although, it is possible that the intention of such meeting may be pure and kind, yet I must tell you such meeting is able to stir up something bad in your spouse.

If there is a necessity for you to have a meeting with an ex-partner, you must specifically seek permission from your spouse. If such permission is granted, it is fair. If such permission is not granted, you have a moral duty to obey your spouse. Again, if such permitted is granted at all, you should make the meeting as public and brief as it can be. It will be unthoughtful spending the whole day with an ex-partner because your husband has given the consent for such encounter. Finally, make an ex-partner an ex-partner indeed. Avoid constant phone calls, social network chats, and any kind of messages.

9. Lack of Discernment in Receiving of Gifts

Following this section of the book, you have learnt that it is not only the bad things that destroy marriages that even some good things may deal a deathblow to marriage. One of such good things that can destroy marriages is receiving of gifts.

I just imagined someone say, "Are you kidding me?"

Let us consider it.

Gifts are not merely material things offered to another party. They convey deep meanings. If these meanings fall on the negative, they can destroy marriages.

Let us consider this fictional example:

> Harry and Megan had promised themselves a great weekend of exploring new things. The sexual life of the marriage had greatly reduced due to work and career. This weekend, they want to make things new again. On Friday night, Megan had already changed into gorgeous underwear. She wanted the escapades to begin immediately when Harry returned from work.

> When Harry returned, he found his wife extremely captivating. After a very passionate kiss, he said, "I love these undies, how much did you spend on them, I will pay you double the money."
>
> Megan's response gave the marriage a deathblow that took a gracious man to save the marriage. "He wouldn't tell me the price he got it. Do you know Smith, my colleague at work? He gave it to me as a gift." Harry was a gentleman. He didn't start an argument. He only picked up his car keys and went to a motel to lodge for the night. He passed three nights at the motel and rejected all calls from family and friends with respect to plea from Megan. The marriage almost suffered a divorce, but Megan apologized, and Harry was compassionate.

Gifts have great meaning. For no reason are you to receive certain kinds of gifts from someone of the opposite sex when in marriage. Imagine the lady in the fiction above. She stooped so low to the point of receiving undies as a gift. That is highly destructive. If someone of the opposite sex gives you some kind of gifts like undies, you have to reject it immediately. If even a female gives you similar gift, you have to reject it immediately. Not all gifts are meant to be received. Some gifts are specifically meant to be rejected.

If an opposite sex gives you expensive gifts such as cars, a house, diamonds, jewelry, or flowers, which may happen, be sure to let your spouse know about it immediately. It is imperative you do so. It is your spouse's consent that will determine whether you will receive the gifts or not.

Finally, gifts have meaning, and you not only have the duty to learn and discern the meaning of every gift, but you also have a duty to discern the motive of the giver. That was exactly Megan's fault. She didn't see the gift from a carnal point of view, and she was highly insensitive to the fact that Smith was implicitly and steadily demanding an affair from her.

10. Official Trips with Opposite Sex

If I am not mistaken, I just heard someone think out loud, "What is bad in an official trip with an opposite sex?"

Once again, we will feed our minds with a story. You will imagine yourself in that fiction and pass your own moral judgment.

> The joy of traveling to London for a five-day official trip has been the new song in the mouth of Harry. He has already told Megan about it, and she has given her consent to that idea. Harry indeed went for the trip and it was the fourth day already. That evening, Megan switched on the television to see the evening news. What she saw was most shocking to her.
>
> There was a robbery in a five-star hotel in London. A lady suffered a light injury. One of the thieves broke her arm when dragging her. Her name was Lynda. It was reported that Lynda and her partner Harry had lodged in that same hotel for four days now.
>
> Megan could not believe her eyes when she saw that the Harry in the news was her husband and that he had been with another woman in the same hotel for four days. Their news showed a video clip of Harry cuddling the distressed Lynda. Megan was in a great rage. She immediately called her lawyer and started filing for a divorce. It was a serious issue.
>
> It was not easy for Harry to convince her that Lynda was his colleague at work, and they had been on the same mission. However, he was able to prove that though they lodged in the same hotel, they were in separate rooms on separate floors. The mistake was forgiven, but the marriage suffered very harsh circumstances with hurtful words from the mouth of Megan.
>
> Megan had given Harry a fair hearing, but not many partners would have been that receptive to learn and investigate. All this could have been avoided if

> Harry had told Megan earlier that he was on that official trip with another female at work. Lynda, on the other hand, had sought the consent of her husband before engaging in the official mission with another man, so there was no issue at all.

If given an official trip by your company with an opposite sex, there is a strict necessity for you to tell your spouse about it. If your spouse does not consent to the trip, you should report back to your company about a change in the sex of partner for the business trip.

Your marriage is the most important thing. It is more important than the company's goals and accomplishments.

11. Disclosure of Hidden Things

Every marriage has accomplishments and things that should stay hidden for some reasons. Perhaps you and your spouse have put some things in the personal and confidential folders. Do not for any reason, disclose these things.

Let us consider this fiction:

> Harry got home with a very great news. He had just sold three properties worth $3,800,000 and for each property, he is entitled to 6 percent. There was a great celebration that day.
>
> Two days later, Harry received a message from a close family friend Andrew. Andrew wanted a loan of $100,000 loan for a business. He claimed the business was a life-changing one.
>
> Harry told him he was not financially in a position to render the loan. Harry was dismayed when he read Andrew's response: "For real? You cannot help? Damn! Life is not like that bro. Megan told Rachel about the $228,000. You need not lie that you are not in a position to help. You could have just said you don't

like being there for a friend. Well, a friend in need is a friend indeed. Peace, bro."

Harry was shocked, remorseful, and angry. He was shocked by the message, remorseful for not being of help to a friend, and above all, he was very angry that his wife disclosed something personal without his consent.

Harry got home that day from work. This time, it was not a celebration. It was a verbal abuse of Megan. He abused Megan all night long. The issue was settled eventually, but the intimacy of the two-family friends had been slightly reduced or injured.

The moral lesson that can be learnt from this is that under no circumstances should a partner disclose accomplishments or personal things in the marriage without the consent of the other partner. In cases when you have already disclosed your personal information to a third party, you can do well to report yourself to your partner. This is required for knowledge.

Proverbs 11:13 also teaches the need to keep secrets. It states: "A talebearer reveals secrets, But he who is of a faithful spirit conceals a matter."

Also, Proverbs 21:23 says, "Whoever guards his mouth and tongue, keeps his soul from troubles."

If Megan had kept her mouth shut and not revealed the accomplishments until consented by Harry, there would have been no issues with Andrew and his wife.

12. Bringing of Social Status into Marital Status

This is a mistake that is hardly spoken of, but it is detrimental to many marriages. People that usually bring their social status into their marriages usually have problems in their home.

You may be a general in the army, you may be the CEO of a company, you may even be the president of a nation, but when you are with your spouse, you should see yourself as a wife or a husband. The implication of bringing the authority you control in the social world into your marriage is to put your spouse as a subject of that authority. It will be wrong for a general to address his wife or husband as though they are soldiers who are inferior in rank to him.

In Hosea, there was a prophecy that reveals the contractual terms of God's union with men. Hosea 2:16 states: "And it shall be, in that day," Says the Lord, "That you will call Me 'My Husband,' And no longer call Me 'My Master.'"

As it has been seen in the above scripture, God wanted a more intimate marriage where His authority as a master and a sovereign Lord is muted for His wife. He wanted His wife to see Him more as a husband and not merely as the master and Lord that He truly is.

Do not let the accolades and awe you receive in the social world get into your head to the point of bringing pride into the marriage. Pride is a very great missile that can destroy even the most solid marital foundation.

Having seen some of the actions that are detrimental to the sanctity of a marital union, the next section contains detriments that are equally weighty in destroying marriages.

Ten Must Dos in Your Marriage

1. Show Love

> And above all things have fervent love for one another, for 'love will cover a multitude of sins.
>
> —1 Peter 4:8

> Her husband … praises her.
>
> —Prov. 31:28

> She who is married cares … how she may please her husband.
>
> —1 Cor. 7:34

> Be kindly affectionate to one another … in honor giving preference to one another.
>
> —Rom. 12:10

Continue—or revive—your courtship into your married life. Successful marriages don't just happen; they must be developed. Don't take one another for granted or the resulting monotony could harm your marriage. Keep your love for one another growing by expressing it to each other; otherwise, love might fade, and you could drift apart. Love and happiness are not found by seeking them for yourself, but rather by giving them to others. So, spend as much time as possible doing things together. Learn to greet each other with enthusiasm. Relax, visit, sightsee, and eat together.

Don't overlook the little courtesies, encouragements, and affectionate acts. Surprise each other with gifts or favors. Try to "out-love" each other. Don't try to take more out of your marriage than you put into it. A lack of love is the biggest destroyer of marriage. There is also a very implausible and incoherent sequence in the social world. This sequence puts the period of courtship as a premarital thing only. Courtship which features learning and observing your partner should not end immediately when the couples are pronounced married. Courtship should continue even in marriage. You should always retain that vibe that is stirred within you when you visit your spouse or spend a weekend or a holiday with your spouse during the premarital days.

2. Avoid Too Many Negatives and Forgive Quickly

> Be angry, and do not sin: do not let the sun go down on your wrath.
>
> —Eph. 4:26

> Confess your trespasses to one another …
>
> —James 5:16

> … forgetting those things which are behind …
>
> —Phil. 3:13

> Be kind to one another, tenderhearted, forgiving one another, even as God in Christ forgave you.
>
> —Eph. 4:32

To remain angry over hurts and grievances—big or little—can be dangerous. Unless addressed in a timely manner, even little problems can become set in your mind as convictions and can adversely affect your outlook on life. This is why God said to let your anger cool before going to bed. Be big enough to forgive and to say, "I'm sorry." After all, no one is perfect, and you are both on the same team, so be gracious enough to admit a mistake when you make it. Besides, making up is a very pleasant experience, with unusual powers to draw marriage partners closer together. God suggests it, and it works!

3. Grow Together
(Having the Same Goals and Vision For the Future)

The destruction of many marriages is simply because there is no vision in the marriage. There is no purpose in the marriage. There is no direction that the couples are heading towards. What a vision does to a marriage is that it gives it reason to be glued. It keeps the partners on their feet to work for the accomplishments of the vision at all times. The time they have for each other is the time they work as one on a common goal.

A mistake people make is that they think it is only sexual relations that makes a marriage well glued. Sexual relationship plays its own part, but the alignment of vision and the task of attaining it makes married partners find more significance in their relationship.

Divorce, malice, and fights in marriage usually come up because there is no social activity or goal that necessitates the couple to always come together. When a woman sees her husband as the most equipped staff of her lifetime investment, she will certainly not want to lose him and the same goes for the husband.

You have to write down your short-term goals, long term goals, aspirations in life and marriage, and above all, you have to commit yourselves to its fulfilment. With all of this, the sense of interdependence will be heightened, and all mistakes will be easily forgiven for the sake of mutual benefit.

If your marriage seems okay but there is no vision for the marriage, and there is no purpose on which the marriage is built, then you must come up with one.

When Moses was leading the people to the Promised Land, it was his vision that made him endure all the hurts and murmurings of the journey. Even when God gave him a free ticket to be saved alone, he had to beg and intercede for the people that constantly frustrate his efforts. This was only because instead of the moral shortcomings of the people, he saw the vision of leading them to the Promised Land as the most essential thing. Vision is a valid driving force of any marriage to its prosperity. Finally, the vision was accomplished. The people did get to the Promised Land (read Ex. 10:14).

4. Love and Respect

> Love suffers long and is kind; love does not envy; love does not parade itself, is not puffed up; does not behave rudely, does not seek its own, is not provoked, thinks no evil; does not rejoice in iniquity, but rejoices in the truth; bears all things, believes all things, hopes all things, endures all things.
>
> —1 Corinthians 13:4–7

> Be kindly affectionate to one another with brotherly love, in honor giving preference to one another.
>
> —Rom. 12:10

Each spouse has a God-given right to certain personal privacies. Do not secretly tamper with each other's wallets or purses, personal email, and other private property unless given permission. Confidence and trust in one another are essential for happiness, so don't check up on each other constantly. Spend less time trying to "figure out" your spouse and more time trying to please her or him. This works wonders.

> Nevertheless, let each one of you in particular so love His own wife as himself, and let the wife see that she respects her husband.
>
> —Eph. 5:33

Marriage is not a prison, so, spouses should give each other voice in marriage. You have not married a dummy, so allow your spouse to contribute his or her perspectives.

Husbands make sure you love and show your love to your wife in every way and wives make sure you respect your own husband in every way.

5. Laugh Frequently

In marriage and life in general, we must learn to laugh and enjoy good times. To be uptight all the time is dangerous, even for your health. A relationship without a time of fun, laughter damages the mind, body, and the ability to love and respect one another. Laughter it is said is the medicine for the soul generally and more so for your marriage. This brings you closer to each other.

6. Communicate Effectively

One of highest forms of communion two people can have is via communication. Communication reveals the intention of the hearts. In a marriage where this essential ingredient is not channeled in the right way, there is bound to be problem. What people don't know is that even when they choose to be silent and ignore sending and receiving words from their partners, they are also communicating messages. For this reason, communication is what people in marriages do to themselves at all time.

To think communication merely begins in speech or writing is to be wrong and narrow in tackling the problem. The starting point of all communication is facial expression, action, gesticulation, and behavior. If all these aspects are negative, even a kind and mild word will have no effect and will not be received. But if all these are in the positive, even a harsh word can easily be forgiven and may be seen as a joke.

Communicate also via gifts; it expresses love. Go on social media and post a beautiful picture of your partner with kind words. Help with the chores. Pick up your phone and greet your partner's relatives. If you get things right at the level of action and behavior, your wrong use of words may be easily forgiven. Also, it is important to use your mouth to express your worries and fears to your partner. You also have to declare your love constantly. By doing that, you are giving the fire of love power to burn vehemently.

7. Trust Each Other

> Husbands love your wives and do not be bitter toward them.
>
> —Col. 3:19

> "Why do you look at the speck in your brother's eye, but do not consider the plank in your own eye?"
>
> —Matt.7:3

> Love suffers long and is kind; love does not envy; love does not parade itself ...
>
> —1 Cor. 13:4

Trust each other absolutely, stop criticizing, nagging, and finding fault in your partner. Your spouse might lack much, but criticism won't help. Expecting perfection will bring bitterness to you and your spouse. Overlook faults and hunt for the good things. Don't try to reform, control, or compel your partner—you will destroy love. Only God can change people. A sense of humor, a cheerful heart, kindness, patience, and affection will banish many of your marriage problems. Try to make your spouse happy rather than good, and the good will likely take care of itself. The secret of a successful marriage lies not in having the right partner, but in being the right partner.

8. Give and Share

Make sure you give, serve, and bless your spouse in every way. Also make sure you share time, love, money, practically everything. Don't have a space where this is yours and it's a no-go area. Give and share everything, especially, when they don't deserve it. It's easy to love when it is easy or when it was "earned."

9. Be Reasonable in Money Matters

> … for God loves a cheerful giver.
>
> —2 Cor. 9:7

Household income should be shared in a marriage, with each partner having the right to spend a certain portion as desired and according to the family budget. Separate bank accounts tend to remove the opportunity to deepen trust, which is vital for a healthy marriage. Money management is a team effort. Both should be involved, but one spouse should take ultimate responsibility. Money management roles should be determined by personal abilities and preferences.

10. Talk Things Over Freely with One Another

> He who disdains instruction despises his own soul …
>
> —Prov. 15:32

> Do you see a man wise in his own eyes? There is more hope for a fool than for him.
>
> —Prov. 26:12

Few things will strengthen your marriage more than open discussions on major decisions. Changing jobs, purchasing something expensive, and other life decisions should involve both husband and wife—differing opinions should be respected. Talking things over together will avoid many blunders that could greatly weaken your marriage. If, after much discussion and earnest prayer, opinions still differ, the wife should submit to her husband's decision, which should be motivated by his deep love for his wife and his responsibility for her well-being. See Ephesians 5:22–25.

THE POWER OF YOUR WORDS

A believer of Jesus Christ that is yet to know the power in the words of his mouth, which is usually symbolized with the tongue, is a joker. When dealing with the words of your mouth, ignorance is not an excuse. A quality knowledge and practice on the capability of your tongue will make your marriage a proof of peace, serenity, happiness, fulfilment, accomplishments, and body gratification.

Let us examine some functions of the word as contained in the Scriptures.

- *Words are foundational.* The word is the beginning and the foundation of all things (success and failure). John 1:1 opens with this truth, "In the beginning was the Word … " If the word of God is the foundation of God's creation then it follows that the word of man is the foundation and beginning of man's creation. Therefore, your success and your failure in life are all rooted in your word.
- *Words are the being of a person.* The word of a person is an inseparable part of the person; it cannot be detached from the person. It comprises the being of the person. John 1:1 expresses this truth. It states: "the Word was with God, and the Word was God." If the Word of God is inseparable from the personality of God and is equivalent with the God-being, then it follows that the word of a man is equivalent to that man himself.
- *Words are creative.* Your word has a creative power. It makes a new existence for a person. It is built with the capacity to originate. Speaking of the creative power of the Word of God, John 1:3 says, "Through him all things were made; without him nothing was made that has been made." As it has been clearly seen, there

was nothing God made that was outside the creative capacity of God's own Word. In the same capacity, there are no circumstances in your world that are outside the creative capacity of your own word.

- *Words have life and light.* There is life and illumination in the word. When your word is rich, there is brightness on your path and your family's path. Describing the characteristics of God's Word, the Scripture says, "In him was life, and that life was the light of all mankind. The light shines in the darkness, and the darkness did not comprehend it" (John 1:4–5). That is the essence of the word of a person. It carries a life that is supposed to be enlightening to all the people around him. There is an affirmation of this in Proverbs 18:21. It states: "Death and life are in the power of the tongue, And those who love it will eat its fruit."
- *Words can command.* The word is a general controller. It commands things to happen in a way. Let us see what James has to say about the word which he symbolized using the tongue. James 3:3–5 states, "Indeed, we put bits in horses' mouths that they may obey us, and we turn their whole body. Look also at ships: although they are so large and are driven by fierce winds, they are turned by a very small rudder wherever the pilot desires. Even so the tongue is a little member and boasts great things." Here, the Bible tells us of how the words of a person controls his whole life. James uses example of how bits are used to control the horses and how rudder is used to control the ships. You have the capacity to use your words to control your life.
- *Words have authority.* Your words are declarative and authoritative even unto the heavens. In Matthew 18:18, Jesus taught His disciples about the power they wield which is manifested in their words. "Assuredly, I say you, whatever you bind on earth will be bound in

> heaven, and whatever you loose on earth will be loosed in heaven."

The Meaning of Words

Having seen the power of the words of a person, I would like to ask you the following question. What is a person's word?

At this point, you have to widen your understanding in the use of natural languages. An incomplete way to think about a person's word or God's Word is to think of "words" in terms of speech only. The implication of this is that the dumb person has no capacity of words. "But those things which proceed out of the mouth come from the heart, and they defile a man" (Matt. 15:18). From the words of Jesus in the book of Matthew, we see that the origin of all the words is the heart. Therefore, that a person is dumb does not mean he cannot originate words.

What then are words?

Another incomplete way to think of the word is to think of the word as the writings only. Words were indeed described in terms of writing, but that is not all that pertains to words.

When "words" are used in the Scriptures, they are used to describe the ideas that make up a person. They are the defining ideas in a person's heart. The mouth only expresses the abundance of the heart.

Jesus is the Word of God. When describing Jesus, the gospel of John uses the Word. A very myopic way to understand this is that Jesus is God's speech or God's writing language. But then, when the Scriptures say Jesus is God's word, what are the Scriptures really saying?

This is a dialogue that happened between Jesus and Philip. It is contained in the gospel of John 14:7–9.

> Jesus: If you really know me, you will know my father as well. From now on, you do know him and have seen him.
>
> Philip: Lord, show us the Father and that will be enough for us.

> Jesus: (Surprised) Don't you know me, Philip, even after I have been among you such a long time? Anyone who has seen me has seen the Father. How can you say, "Show us the Father"?

What Jesus Christ is saying here is that I am the representation of God. I am the description of His makeup. I am what He is made up of. I am the expression of His reality.

Hebrews 1:3 also affirms to the same truth when it states concerning Jesus Christ that, "The Son is the radiance of God's glory and the exact representation of His being, sustaining all things by the power of His word" (KJV).

Now, we can see what is meant by your word. There are some bad mental images that people have of themselves. These images which may be expressed in speech, writing, and action has a way to depict who the person is. Also, it creates a reality for the person.

So, in addition to your words, also guard your thoughts.

> For as he thinks in his heart, so is he.
>
> —Prov. 23:7

> Keep your heart with all diligence, for out of it spring the issues of life.
>
> —Prov. 4:23

> Whatever things are true … noble … just … pure … lovely … of good report … meditate on these things.
>
> —Phil. 4:8

You will agree with me that the wrong kind of thinking can profoundly harm your marriage. The devil will tempt you with thoughts like, "Our marriage was a mistake," "She doesn't understand me," "I can't take much more of this," "We can always divorce if necessary," "I'll go home to mother," or, "He smiled at that woman." This kind of thinking is dangerous because your thoughts ultimately govern your actions. Avoid seeing, saying, reading, or hearing anything that—or associating with anyone who—suggests being unfaithful. Thoughts uncontrolled are like an automobile left in neutral on a steep hill; the result could be a disaster.

For this reason, we are going to examine some mental pictures and images that people usually conceive in their mind that is detrimental not only to their marriage but to their life also.

Destructive Mental Images and Words That Must Be Eliminated

"I am such a failure."

Is that you? Your word which is the fullness of your reality must not be this. It is abominable that all you conceive about yourself is this. If this is what you have been thinking, then you must immediately be transformed. The Scripture says, "Yet in all these things we are more than conquerors through Him who loved us." (Rom. 8:37)

You must immediately begin to see yourself as a victor as expressed in your reality. Find your reality in the word of God and not in earthly circumstances.

1 Peter 1:23 tells you expressly that, "having been born again, not of corruptible seed but incorruptible, through the word of God which lives and abides forever."

Henceforth, you have a duty to open the Scriptures and search out your reality in the Word of God through which you are born. You must fill your hearts with the words of these verses. With this, you will see all-around transformation in your life, in your marriage, in your academic pursuits and all other endeavors of life.

"I should be able to do that."

What exactly should you be able to do? If it is the negative things according to the standards of this world, then you should not do it. The world tells you when you are facing a powerful challenge in your marriage, you can call for a legal dissolution of that marriage.

That is what the natural laws of this world tells you, but the law of God does not want you to conform to the standards of the earth. Romans 12:2 teaches us this clearly. It states: "Do not be conformed to this world, but be transformed by the renewal of your mind, that by testing you may know what is the will of God, what is good and acceptable and perfect."

You have learnt to extract and eliminate all standards that do not agree with God's word from your heart. Your reality and mental images should be exactly corresponding to God's word.

Although, the world validates homosexuality, bestiality, divorce, and even suicide, you must not in any way let all these decadences of ideas find expression through you. In the world we live in today, this notion is not the norm. But I believe in the Bible, so, if you have issues with this stand please take it with God not me because I didn't write the Bible.

"This always happens to me."

Some people are the product of people's wrong perception about them. Are you a wife that always wakes up to the words of a husband pointing out all the wrongs you have done the prior day? All some people hear are their mistakes and failures in life. In a most surrendering state of mind, they have taken this as the norm of their life.

Finally, when they find themselves doing the same thing that was identified with them, they express from the abundance of their heart: "This always happens to me, I always lose things that are special to me."

Whatever people say about you, your mistakes in life and the errors you make as a human being are not your reality.

There are certainly people that have told you, "you can never be a good husband." There are people that have told you, "You will always fight in your marriage." There are people that have studied your hurtful pasts and predicted your disastrous future to your very own face. In times past, you might have been a victim of this negative prediction. However, I am thrilled to tell you today that you are free. You are blessed. You are the excellence of this world. The plan of God for you is to succeed in life, including your marriage.

Isaiah 54:17 says to you that:

> No weapon formed against you shall prosper, And every tongue which rises against you in judgment. You shall condemn. This is the heritage of the servants of the Lord, And their righteousness is from Me, says the Lord.

First, the Scripture tells you that all negative talks about you will not prosper. Second, you have a duty to condemn such negative thought. Condemn every thought that says you will fail. Third, the Scripture tells you of a new heritage that you have acquired. Lastly, the Scripture describes the heritage. The heritage is Jesus' righteousness. It is yours. If the world calls you a failure, a pauper, and a sinner, you remind them of your new heritage, and you walk in that newness. Be transformed to transform.

"I feel so guilty."

Are you that person that has been overwhelmed with a feeling of guilt and the errors of the past? Has that been your self-created reality? You must destroy such words and images from your heart.

Have you traced the cessation of your past marriage to yourself? You believe you are the cause of all the misfortune in your world. What guilt does is it strips you naked in your own eyes and constantly bugs you with a thought of indignity. Guilt tells you, "You are not worthy of good things."

Now, the causal factors of guilt can be traced to errors made in the past to God and to men. Some people accept calamities in their life acknowledging that God is punishing them from all the errors and sins of the past. Is this you? If yes, listen carefully to what God has to say to you.

The book of Psalms expresses God's verdict concerning you. Psalm 103:12 says, "As far as the east is from the west, so far has he removed our transgressions from us." With this, you can see that God has greatly detached you from those past that hurt you. There are two things that cannot meet in any possible sense. It is the east and the west cardinal points. They face different directions and so they do not have any contact whatsoever. Also, you have been detached from all those sins and mistakes of the past that keep haunting you. If it's true that you have been liberated from all sins, why should you be so cruel to yourself by bearing the pain of the sin? Let all the feeling of guilt die and never be raised again.

The Scripture has declared something new about you. 2 Corinthians 5:17 states, "Therefore, if anyone is in Christ, he is a new creature; old things have passed away; behold, all things have become new." He has destroyed all your old and past nature; He has made you a whole new creature.

You, guilty man or woman! How do you think God views you? Let us see the book of Psalms and see what he has to say concerning His saints. Psalm 16:3 states, "As for the saints who are on the earth, they are the excellent ones in whom is all my delight." As it has been clearly seen, God has found His delight in your being. You need not condemn yourself. However, if there is any way you think you are getting it wrong, you can just go to Him in prayer and ask for grace and help in times of need.

"I am not good enough."

In marriages, many people still suffer from low esteem. They believe they are not as worthy to be in that relationship with respect to beauty, career, educational standards, and wealth. This is a humility unto the destruction of not only the marriage but to the self. Everyone has his own weakness, however, to pass a condemnation verdict on yourself for your own weaknesses is very unfair.

In 2 Corinthians 12:9, the great apostle Paul made a brief comment on how he dealt with his weakness. He said: "And He has said to me, 'My grace is sufficient for you, for my strength is made perfect in weakness. Therefore, most gladly I will rather boast in my infirmities, that the power of Christ may rest upon me.'"

From the passage, we can learn that the apostle went to God directly in prayer and he did receive word not for himself only but for all people limiting themselves too. It is a fact that you are always good enough for God's noble use. In spite of your weakness, God is ready to do great and mighty things with you. You are just good enough and complete for any outstanding marital success. You have to give yourself a quality perception of yourself.

"This marriage can't work." or "This marriage sucks."

As it has been learnt, the word of a person is not only creative but also declarative. It has the power to produce real life results that it is identical to it. It is this principle that makes the Word of God (Christ) identical with God. The word of a person is the exact representation of a person's mind and the express image of that person.

If all that is contained in your mind and your word are the images of a failed and precarious marriage, then such image must not find expression in your heart. Also, such words as "This marriage can't work, this marriage sucks, I want out. I am out of love. I am so done," must not find expression in your mouth.

THE DS THAT ARE THE DEMONS OF A BAD MARRIAGE

There is a new wave of knowledge that many people fail in life and marriage because they could not accurately discern whom their enemy is and what they are up against. I absolutely agree with this line of thought. During counseling sessions, people are asked the number one problem or enemy they have in their marriage. They then start telling you funny characters like "He" or "She." By "he," the wife is saying the husband is the only reason why the marriage won't work and by "she," the husband is also saying vice versa. What nonsense! If your spouse is the number one enemy of your marriage, who then are we struggling to get the marriage right for? A more modest and common answer that people give is "his sister, his brother, his mum, his dad, her sister, her brother, her mum, or her dad." If you think this is the reason why your marriage is not working, then you have got it all wrong.

The book of Ephesians is indeed an eye-opener to a very significant truth. Ephesians 6:11–12 states:

> Put on the whole armor of God, that you may be able to stand against the wiles of the devil. For we do not wrestle against flesh and blood, but against principalities, against powers, against the rulers of the darkness of this age, against spiritual hosts of wickedness in the heavenly places.

As it is written and clearly understood, our enemy is not something natural. It is not natural human beings. What confronts us in our marriage and life generally is something spiritual. Something that is more exceedingly powerful than natural men. We are confronted by an evil that is determined to have our homes and relationship destroyed. Without doubt, the only enemy in your marriage is the devil.

Having seen our enemy naked, let us delve into the Scriptures and acquire some facts about the ideas and mental images he is made up of. I don't have time to waste on the devil because he is a loser. This subsequent section will be brief.

The Devil's Mental Make-Up

Killing and Lying

While Jesus Christ was declaring that those who do not believe in him are under the patriarchy of the devil, he revealed an important trait of the devil. John 8:44 states, "You are of your father the devil, and the desires of your father you want to do. He was a murderer from the beginning, and does not stand in the truth, because there is no truth in him. When he speaks a lie, he speaks from his own resources, for he is a liar and the father of it."

This verse is explicit and easy to understand. That being is a murderer and a lie. He is determined to murder that beautiful marriage of yours with his own language which are all lies.

Hindering of Prosperity

Another of Satan's major degree is to hinder the prosperity of every good and pleasing things. He is skilled in hindering the prosperity of a marriage. Paul made a comment on his nature in 1 Thessalonians 2:18. It states, "Therefore we wanted to come to you—even I, Paul, time and again—but Satan hindered us."

He is ready to block all marriages from being accomplished, successful, and celebrated.

Evil Influence

The devil is skilled in crawling as a serpent into people's heart and poisoning it with evil counsel. John 13:2 authenticates this act of the devil. It states, "And supper being ended, the devil having already put it into the heart of Judas Iscariot, Simon's son, to betray Him."

In the same fashion, the devil is still at work today prompting spouses to be problematic to their partner. It would take more than a millennium to write out the cruelty in the mind of the devil. We need not waste such a time on him.

Jesus Christ has concluded by saying, "The thief does not come except to steal, and to kill, and to destroy. I have come that they may have life, and that they may have it more abundantly" (John 10:10).

The devil is destruction-personified. All he does is to destroy. For this reason, any divorce, fights, problems, disconnection can all be traced to him.

Talking about the devil without reminding you of the good news is an incomplete fact. Once again, you should be reminded that although the devil exists in his own kingdom, the Scriptures speak of God and His kingdom. It says, "For he has rescued from the dominion of darkness and brought us into the kingdom of the son he loves."

With the quality knowledge of the new kingdom, you have a duty to abide by the constitution of that kingdom through obeying and using the standards of Christ's marriage with the church.

The Damage the Devil Does to Your Marriages

Here, we will take you through some words that begin with letter D. That these words begin with D's are not coincidental, they are specifically used because D stands for the devices of the devil towards the destruction of every good thing and marriage.

In 2 Corinthians 2:11, the Scriptures say, "Lest Satan should get an advantage of us; for we are not ignorant of his devices." In the strength of that Scripture, I also say, we are not ignorant of the devices of the dreams of the devil concerning our marriage. Learn from them and avoid that such devices take charge in your own marriage. Look closely at these D's and you will find that any of the categories reflects where you are in your marriage but be determined to change it and abide by God's model of marriage. Be committed to keeping your relationship fresh and alive.

Distance

People usually think dissolution of marriage is achieved by the mere event of putting signature on the paper. This is not so. Many marriages have been long dissolved by the devil. People just see the manifestation of such dissolution when the marriage finally crumbles. A major way the devil achieves this is to set in a great distance between husbands and wives.

Be careful not to misunderstand what I mean by this. By distance, I do not mean physical distance. The husband may be in America and the wife in Europe, and yet they remain absolutely connected and glued together.

By distance, what is meant is that the devil's foundational device is to set a mental barrier between the husband and wife. He makes their hearts oceans, planet, seas, and universes grow apart.

In the early days, the distance may begin with husband forgetting important days like birthdays, wedding anniversary, graduation anniversary, and all of that. Then at its peak, people may totally forget each other's name. In this stage, there is no use of romantic terms like, "Honey, Darling, Sweetheart, or Love," let alone natural names like "Joshua, Felicia, Cole, and Malia." Couples at this stage usually address themselves mostly using pronouns like, "you, she, or he."

To see how deeply the termite of "Distance" can eat into a marriage. Let us consider this fiction.

> The kitchen is absolutely out of use.
>
> Harry and Megan had not really been getting along well. On work days, they both eat at restaurants and buy food on their way back from work. On weekends, Harry goes out with his friends all day long, and Megan sorts herself out. Of course, they have both agreed on separate bedrooms.
>
> That Saturday, Harry's friends decided to throw him a surprise visit as early 10:00 a.m. They decided to spend the weekend at his house.
>
> Megan opened the door to welcome the unexpected guests. She went up to notify Harry of his guests downstairs. She knocked several times, but Harry would not open. She then went downstairs angrily to report Harry to his friends.

Surprised that Harry would not open his door to his wife even after multiple knocks, Jack picked up his cell and called Harry.

These were Harry's words: "Are you kidding me, home boy? Are you really around? It would have been a great weekend. But I have been in Washington D.C. since Monday."

Jack would have doubted it if there had not been a loud vehicle sound at the background. Obviously, he was not in his room. He gave Megan and Smith, the other friend, the report, and they left.

Megan was home alone crying all day long and all night long. She knew she had already lost her marriage by the devil's device of distance.

This is how the devil dreams about your marriage. He is ready to distance you from your spouse. Now, that you are aware of his devices, forgive any offense. Commune with your spouse. Love and listen to your spouse. Do not give distance preeminence over your relationship.

Dissatisfaction

Why do you think Megan was crying? She was displeased about herself, her marriage, and in her husband. She had lost all hope and was greatly weakened by disappointment.

The devil is committed to using this device to hurt her and to make her continue in that misery. Dissatisfaction will not give her a way forward. It will only keep telling her the things she did wrong. And more than her own flaws, the devil will make her absolutely and totally give up on her partner and her marriage. She may begin to think, *Why did I even get myself into this mess? What image of me will Smith and Jack have? What has Harry been telling them about me? What kind of man will travel for six days without calling his wife or informing his wife? Obviously, this thing is not a man but an animal.* All of these are the devices of the devil for your life. It is designed to keep you trapped in the confines of that darkness and to stir up blame from the two parties in the relationship.

On the other hand, Harry might also be wondering, What kind of woman would not call her husband for six days? I am just stuck in this relationship. I must just free myself.

Whenever you are overwhelmed by guilt and dissatisfaction, please pick up your Bible. At that point, you need to see yourself with the lens of God and not your natural lens. The word of God says you are the righteousness of God in Christ. The word of God says you are His eternal excellency. By seeing yourself and your husband as God sees the two of you, you can free yourself from the confines of self-guilt and displeasure at the action of others. It is a whole new stage of the devil that is very destructive to the married. You must see yourselves at this point as "Works of God" in progress. By this, you can have less or no displeasure of or for yourselves.

Discouragement

This is another aspect of the big devil's dream concerning the destruction of all marriages. All glory to God that the enemy's plans have failed already.

> Megan had wept all night long. It was Sunday morning, but she could not bring herself up to prepare for church. Her heart was just too heavy. All night, she could not bring herself to sleep for five minutes. All through the night, she had great deliberation within herself. She concluded that she would call Harry this morning and ask about his welfare and arrival period. She made a hot coffee.
>
> Just as she was about to pick up her phone and make the call, the devil deceived her saying, "Why should you call a man who didn't tell you where he was or when he was leaving? By calling him, you make yourself look weak and broken. This is a man that doesn't care about your own state. He has not called to apologize for his mistake. Who knows? He might be in a hotel room with one of those demonic girls."

> She dropped her phone overwhelmed by the discouragement of the devil. She was absolutely ignorant of the devices of the devil.

Discouragement is like a rope to draw people back. When Paul said "Satan hindered us" in his letter to the Thessalonians, he meant that Satan discouraged them. He discouraged the great apostles, and he is still in the business of discouraging people today. He tied that rope to Megan's heart and just when she was about to make a good move, discouragement drew her backwards.

Be not discouraged. Irrespective of all that has happened, be the first to make that move. Be the first to say you are sorry. Be the first to establish a reconciliation, for ours is the ministry of reconciliation. Be the first to ask for forgiveness even though you opine that you are not wrong.

Disengagement

The dream of the devil for the destruction of the marriage includes absolute disengagement between the wife and the husband. By setting their hearts apart, he has already made them disconnect at the level of the heart. But the devil is not yet satisfied; he wants more. He wants them to totally disengage at the level of their declaration to the world. He wants them to start telling people in their social world that we are no longer together. He wants them to start professing their disengagement to the world. Let us see how the devil became successful in spelling the disengagement through Megan.

> It was a painful weekend. Megan had risen from weeping to being filled with hatred and anger for Harry. On that Monday morning, she cleaned herself up for work. As she got to work, there were greetings from here and there: "Good morning Mrs. Marshal." She hardly responded. It was obvious something was wrong. She headed straight to her office. She was displeased by her action of not responding to the greetings from her coworkers. She exhaled heavily and went back to the hall. She screamed, "I am very sorry for the

attitude I displayed when coming in. I am sincerely sorry. But I just want to officially beg you all not to call me 'Mrs. Marshal' for now. I am okay with Megan only. Yes, Megan."

Wow! That was a hot cake for the gossips. Megan had just given the breaking news. The whole world now knows she is disengaged or separating from her husband. At this point, the devil could be seen rejoicing that his great dream is being accomplished. It is impending that the marriage will crumble. They were absolutely ignorant of the devices of the devil. They are disconnected, and the whole world is now focusing on them.

Disharmony

The disharmony between husband and wife is a significant part of the whole dream. With a heart filled with lies, hatred, grudges, animosity, and utmost displeasure, the devil has already created a good platform for a serious fight. The disharmony usually happens after series of hatred fully matured in their hearts.

On that Monday evening, Megan got back from work pretty late. She had taken her time to be busy with things at work trying to take her mind off everything.

As she got home, she saw that the light in the living room had been switched on. She thought to herself, "The idiot must be back." Suddenly, she opened her bag, picked up her phone and called 911, reporting that a stranger seem to have broken into her apartment. In the twinkle of an eye, the police was around and the whole atmosphere was not looking calm anymore. Megan had been taken into a police car.

Harry came out to see what the sirens were all about. Immediately, as he opened the door; he was apprehended by two police men. All efforts to tell them that he didn't know what was happening proved futile. However, in about a moment, Megan came out of the

> vehicle and testified that he was a member of the house and that she had reasons to think it was a stranger because he had not been around for a time now. The police took some reports and drove off.
>
> What followed after that was serious. It was a night of loud arguments and verbal abuses. Just at about midnight, Megan called Harry "a dog who has been sleeping around with all the girls." Of course, her words provoked a heavy slap.
>
> That was the end. Megan picked up her car keys and drove away. She was done.

At this stage, the devil introduces a dispute to finally tear them apart. If the couples could not be counseled through this stage, what follows is the paperwork, what follows is getting the attorneys involved, which will later result in divorce.

In the Megan-Harry case, it is already apparent that the marriage had long been broken from the time they had been mentally distanced from each other. They were susceptible to the destructive power of the devil. They were ignorant of the devil and his devices. They saw an enemy in their respective selves; meanwhile they never faced and tackled the true enemy via prayer and godly counsel.

Divorce

At this stage, the devil's dream has finally been achieved. All the important documents have been signed. The marriage has been canceled in the eyes of the law. Megan and Harry have become ex-partners.

Their kind of marriage could not stand the missiles of the devil because it was not shielded with the ark of God which is Jesus Christ. It was founded upon the dreams and devices of the devil. These include lies, unforgiveness, animosity, lack of honor, and guilt. Megan and Harry did indeed divorce and the devil did indeed have reasons to celebrate them.

Having seen the devices of the devil to the destruction of lives and marital homes, there is more to see. Let us see where the loopholes were created for the devil to creep in. Along the line, something must have gone wrong. Marriage is between two people who once swore their adoration to themselves. If that oath is broken, then there must be a cause to that. In the next section, you will be learning about the problems of marriage that are man-made.

COMMON PROBLEMS IN MARRIAGE

To attribute all problems in marriage to the devil is to be narrow in scope. There are spiritual problems in marriage that are rooted in the power of the devil. On the other hand, there are also man-made problems that are rooted in the denial of certain marital rights. This section will highlight three of such man-made problems and give practical solutions to them.

Lack of Communication

One of highest forms of communion two people can have is via communication. Communication reveals the intention of the hearts. In a marriage where this essential ingredient is not channeled in the right way, there is bound to be problem. What people don't know is that even when they choose to be silent and ignore sending and receiving words from their partners, they are also communicating messages. For this reason, communication is what people in marriages do to themselves at all time.

To think communication merely begins in speech or writing is to be wrong and narrow in tackling the problem. The starting point of all communication is a facial expression, an action, a gesticulation, and a behavior. If all these aspects are negative, even a kind and mild word will have no effect and will not be received. But if all these are in the positive, even a harsh word can easily be forgiven and may be seen as a joke.

Always smile at your partner. Communicate via gifts; it expresses love. Go on social media and post a beautiful picture of your partner with kind words. Help with the chores. Pick up your phone and greet your partner's relatives. If you get things right at the level of action and behavior, your wrong use of words may be easily forgiven. Also, it is important to use your mouth to express your worries and fears to your partner.

Let us take a reference back of the Megan-Harry divorce of the last chapter. The devil was doing his whole part of tempting and deceiving them and the other hand, they were making a grave mistake of not communicating. If there had been communication on the trip, things might have not been so catastrophic.

Lack of Vision

The word of God in Habakkuk 2:2 expresses a very important truth. It states: "And the Lord answered me, and said, Write the vision, and make it plain upon tables, that he may run that readeth it."

The destruction of many marriages is simply because there is no vision in the marriage. There is no purpose in the marriage. There is no direction that the couples are heading towards. What a vision does to a marriage is that it gives it reason to be glued. It keeps the partners on their feet to work for the accomplishments of the vision at all times. The time they have for each other is the time they work as one on a common goal.

A mistake people make is that they think it is only sexual relations that make a marriage well glued. Sexual relationship plays its own part, but the alignment of vision and the task of attaining it makes married partners find significance in their relationship more.

Divorce, malice, and fights in marriage usually come up because there is no social activity or goal that necessitates the couple to always come together.

You have to write down your short-term goals, long-term goals, aspirations in life and marriage, and above all, you have to commit yourselves to its fulfilment. With all of this, the sense of interdependence will be heightened, and all mistakes will be easily forgiven for the sake of mutual benefit.

If your marriage seems okay but there is no vision for the marriage, and there is no purpose on which the marriage is built, then you must come up with one.

When Moses was leading the people to the Promised Land, it was his vision that made him endure all the hurts and murmurings of the journey. Even when God gave him a free ticket to be saved alone, he had to beg and intercede for the people that constantly frustrated his efforts. This was only because instead of the moral shortcomings of the people, he saw the vision of leading them to the Promised Land as the most essential thing. Vision is a valid driving force of any marriage to its prosperity. Finally, the vision was accomplished. The people did get to the Promised Land (read Ex. 10:14).

Lack of Sex

Sexual relationship is as important in marriage as much as water is as important to the body. Just like oxygen is important to the human body, sex is important in every marriage.

> Let the husband render to his wife the affection due her, and likewise also the wife to her husband. The wife does not have authority over her own body, but the husband does. And likewise, the husband does not have authority over his own body, but the wife does. Do not deprive one another except with consent for a time, that you may give yourselves to fasting and prayer; and come together again so that Satan does not tempt you because of your lack of self-control. But I say this as a concession, not as a commandment.
>
> —1 Corinthians 7:3–6

As it has been seen, the Scriptures also affirm the need for sex. Therefore, sex should not be denied on the ground of "I want to be holy for God." Your husband and your wife owns your body. Even if there is a need to pray and fast, ensure you take consent from your spouse before doing so. And as the writer of Corinthians says, this should not take too much time.

In cases where the lack of sex is because the husband and wife are not just connecting anymore or aroused by the other anymore, there is a more serious problem. This level of sexual denial in marriage can be traced to communication. Ensure you communicate to your spouse in various languages that is most appealing to them. If her language is receiving gifts, then you should do so. If what always makes him smile is when you sing alone for him, then don't deny him that pleasing voice. Do all that is required to ensure that your affections are communicated via touch, words, behavior, and facial expression.

Let us see some sexual requirements that must be met to make your sexual life beautiful again.

The Perceptual Requirement

This is also a very important requirement to a fulfilling sexual life. If you are a woman and your hair looks rough with lice and you have body odor, you are destroying your sex life and marriage gradually. If you are a man and your beard and hair are not well trimmed and shaved, you are also doing the same. Ensure you give your quality self for your spouse to see. Ensure you put on clean and sexually driving underwear. Also, wear good perfume that makes you smell nice.

The Environmental Requirement

It is true that atmosphere and environment play vital roles in ensuring a good and fulfilled sex life. Ensure your bedroom is well kept with clean and beautiful bed sheets. Apply a quality air freshener in your bedroom. A good environment gives a good sensation. A good sensation produces the right mental platform for sex.

The Entertainment Requirement

This aspect may be skipped depending on the couples. You can get a romantic movie or play quality blues songs. A romantic movie will help soften your hearts and prepare for that beautiful time.

The Disciplinary Requirement

One of the problems of partners that causes cessation of sex in marriages is when the partners are not disciplined in their relationship with the opposite sex. No woman will be happy to commune with a cheating husband and vice versa or perceived to be cheating because of flirting with the opposite sex. Therefore, unless you begin to discipline yourself in your relationship with the opposite sex, your sex life will remain injured. Having seen a practical solution to some artificial problems of marriage, let us see the final status that your marriage should take.

Marriage Should Be Celebrated

> You are the light of the world. A city that is set on a hill cannot be hidden. Nor do they light a lamp and put it under a basket, but on a lampstand, and it gives light to all who are in the house. Let your light so shine before men, that they may see your good works and glorify your Father in heaven.
>
> —Matthew 5:14–16

Here God wants us to show the world the perfection of our marriage. Let people learn from your marriage. Celebrate your marriage and family and let men glorify God for His love in your home. A good marriage is not something that should be hidden. Let people hear your testimony about your marriage.

There are many testimonies that abound about how my marriage and ministry has been a blessing and inspiration to others. I do not glory in all of this, but I glory in the marriage and family of God that is the original version I built my family from. The marriage and family of God is the foundation upon which I am established. Let people see your marriage and be blessed.

Finally, remember that your marriage is created to exemplify or reveal the marriage of Christ to the church. This is marriage of an everlasting love and unbreakable covenants. This is who we are and who we should strive to be. The marriage of Christ should be your number one study guide and reference material for the glorious end you desire. This contractual term of this marriage is richly contained in this book. A consistent study and practice of its content will surely guarantee your triumph in life and marriage. Also, learn from all the stories that were shared in the book with a commitment to reorienting yourselves. Remember that the only enemy of your marriage is not your spouse or anyone else but the devil. Therefore, channel your prayer and war against the real enemy. Remain blessed and triumphant.

All marriages have a knot to which they are tied; family is the expressive aspect of all marriages. The next section of this book is richly furnished with the knowledge needed to establish your family on a solid and prosperous ground.

FAMILY: THE SEED OF ALL MATRIMONY

You cannot talk of marriage without talking about family. God wanted a family. He created Adam and Eve to start this family. The reality of having beautiful seeds is that you can show the foundation of what you cherish; my family is blessed to have me as theirs. They have reasons to indeed learn from my marriage because it reflects the marriage of Christ.

Sociology posits that the family is an integral part of the society. For what it is worth, the family is the foundation and the place from which a person learns most of the things that constitute his personality. It then makes sense that something that is pivotal should not be left void of the counsel and the will of God. For every marriage, there is a family. As one is faced with two parties only, the other comprise of two or more parties. This makes it all the more salient. Every family usually faces problems of its own. Again, irrespective of how you feel, you have to know and be resolute that you will not cut the anchor of the family that holds the society together. In the midst of hardship and pain, we can rely on the Bible for the stability, guidance, and security we need. Sometimes we go through difficult times in our lives. Like ships in a storm, we can be tossed around by the wind, needing help to remain stable. The family is an anchor that will never fail. Just like Paul in Acts 27:29, to avoid shipwreck, they casted four anchors, and we should too. In this chapter, our focus will be on the family as an anchor that never fails.

Main Idea

The plan of God for the family still stands; this is an anchor that helps stabilize you from the storm of life e.g. marital storms. Joshua 24:15 says:

> And if it seems evil to you to serve the Lord, choose for yourselves this day whom you will serve, whether the

> gods which your fathers served that were on the other side of the River, or the gods of the Amorites, in whose land you dwell. But as for me and my house, we will serve the Lord.

The Family

Like an anchor holds a ship, our hope in the family guarantees our safety. Whatever the conditions at sea, the anchor is to remain fixed on the bottom of the sea. The first institution God created was the family, even before the church. We need this institution to be healthy and to function, as ordained by God. The truth is the family institute is under constant attack by the devil because he recognizes the importance of the family in society. Understandably, the decadence being witnessed in the society at large is a result of the destruction of the family.

The family is to be a union between a man and woman, not a man and a man or woman and woman. The family unit is under attack, and people are scared to now speak against this. Irrespective of what the society thinks or accepts as right, the Word of God remains true.

It was the devil that came to destroy the family in Genesis 3. He knows that if he can destroy the family; he can destroy the society. The family comprises of man, woman, kids, and others.

Who Is Your Family?

Our Lord Jesus Christ gave an answer to this question in this dialogue as contained in Matthew 12:47–50:

> Someone: "Your mothers and brothers are standing outside, wanting to speak to you."
>
> Jesus: "Who is my mother, and who are my brothers? (pointing to His disciples) Here are my mother and my brothers."

There are so many things to learn from Jesus' perspective of family. While He didn't deny explicitly that His biological family is His family, He extended the chain of family membership to His disciples. If this is so, we can say that people who have done the will of your father (God) by obeying the gospel of Jesus are your family members.

However, our focal area in this chapter is not merely the wide and universal family but the social family. This social family will consist of wife, husband, children, and all fellows under the parental leadership of the father and mother.

Family: The God-Given Anchor

The family is your anchor, and God's plan is to use the family as a formidable means of stability. If you're struggling in this area, irrespective of how you feel, the family working together will help stabilize you in times of storm. In this section, attention will be vested on only the parental aspect of the family which is comprised of husband and wife.

Jesus even made sure that His first miracle was at a wedding; He seems to be saying that you destroyed the first family, but I will restore it back to His glory. He will start restoring what the devil destroyed.

What is God's Idea of a Godly Family?

Although society has been on a campaign to deface the role of husbands/fathers as head of the family, it's a responsibility bestowed by God himself, but be reminded husbands, you are to act as leaders, and this role is of responsibility not that of "lording or superiority." Just like Joshua said in Joshua 24:15 "… but as for me and my house, we'll serve the Lord."

Don't let your wife do all the tasks of raising the family, praying, etc. God has tasked the husband to lead and He holds the husband responsible.

Somebody has to lead. You must have heard often nowadays that we shouldn't spank our children. "Let them learn the correct way," people say.

"Spare the rod and spoil the child." Proverbs 22:15 says, "Foolishness is bound up in the heart of a child; the rod of correction will drive it far from him."

The application of the rod should not be applied abusively but responsibly. Don't be too harsh on the kids and don't break their spirit. Proverbs 29:15 says: "The rod and rebuke give wisdom, but a child left to himself brings shame to his mother."

He who the Lord loves He chastened, so if you love your child you should correct them with love. Jesus loves the church, so be to your family how Jesus is to the church.

Issues That Have Weakened Traditional Families

The frequency of the decision "to marry and stay married" has steadily declined over the past few decades. Cohabitation, non-marital childbearing, and childlessness are all increasing rapidly. The divorce rate is skyrocketing daily as well as the rigid freedom of immature children to do what they like is having a negative impact on the family and society.

The state involvement in raising children against God's wishes in the Bible is prevalent.

The satanic attacks on the family are the continuation of what Satan started in Genesis 3.

The state's interference in marriage is another prevailing nuisance for the weakening of families. Laws encouraging divorce has indirectly conditioned a section of the divide to easily seek divorce at will in marriages.

The good news: Irrespective of all these issues, the next generation is still interested in the institution of marriage and the family. Many still believe that marriage is an important and relevant institution.

Marriage is the bedrock of family as Jesus is the bedrock of marriage.

Four Reasons Why God Relies on the Family

Read Genesis 2:18–25. This is the foundation of a great marriage.

Marriage is an Institution Ordained by God (v. 18–19)

The first thing we have to understand is that God created marriage. There are two institutions God created: the family and the church.

One of the main purposes of marriage is companionship. It's built for companionship and for that person to be your best friend. I want you to notice in these verses that God told Adam to name every animal. But why? Because he wanted to see Adam's need. He wanted to see how he would use the mandate given to him. As Adam named the creatures, he saw two animals coming, one of each kind, e.g., Mr. and Mrs. Elephant, Mr. and Mrs. Giraffe, and Adam may have been thinking, "There are two of everyone except me."

But "Two are better than one, because they have a good return for their work" (Eccl. 4:9). One of the biggest mistakes couples make is thinking that marriage is supposed to be easy and they may think that since it's difficult at times, that God must not be in it. Instead, God created marriage because there's a need for companionship that we all have. There's another reason for this companionship.

Marriage is Supposed to Make You Christ-like

It's His way of transforming you into the person He wants you to become. In his famous passage on marriage, Paul talks about the roles of men and women; how each by fulfilling their roles gives us a picture of Jesus and His transforming power.

"For this reason, a man will leave his father and mother and be joined to his wife, and the two will become one flesh" (Eph. 5:31). It's only God who can do this.

This is a quote from Genesis 2, but Paul introduces it to show that everything a man is supposed to do and everything a woman is supposed to do is geared towards becoming like Jesus. Too many times the reason marriages struggle is because we have the wrong idea of the purpose of marriage.

Marriage Will Not Complete You (v. 20–21)

You may not agree with this point, but let's see it from this point of view. Normal mathematics have two halves equaling a whole, right? That's not how relationships work.

Two incomplete people in a relationship equals two incomplete people, and two complete people equals wholeness in a relationship. The myth or the illusion is this: "My marriage is supposed to complete me." I understand why we believe this since our society and everything around is telling us this. Isn't it romantic to believe you're incomplete without someone?

In verse 24, we'll read that "two become one flesh," not two halves equal one.

Why is this important?

Because when a person believes they are incomplete and marriage will complete them, it puts pressure on their marriage that their marriage was never meant to bear. So that when your spouse doesn't make you feel complete, the problem appears to be your spouse because you have the notion that marriage should complete you.

Great marriages involve two complete people becoming one. Anything less is a fraction, and fraction marriages have problems. There is a place to go to be complete, but it's not your spouse, it's Jesus. Make Jesus first in your marriage, i.e., the third person of the Trinity and behold Him. As you do that you both will get closer to Jesus, hence the transformation.

> And you are complete in Him, who is the head of all principality and power.
>
> —Col. 2:10

Jesus completes people, not marriage; that's what Jesus wants.

Marriage is Knowing You're the Right Person (v. 22–23)

I know a lot of people run to dating sites to find the right person. But the challenge is there's no website helping us become the right person. God created Eve and presented her to Adam as his helper. Now before you get thoughts of helper as some kind of assistant, this Hebrew word "helper," ezer kenegdo in Hebrew, is mostly used of God as a helper.

In Exodus 18:4, Moses named one of his sons Eliezer, which in Hebrew means, "My God is my helper" (Eli = "my God"; ezer = "helper").

This verse goes on to explain why Moses named his son Eliezer: because God had powerfully delivered Moses from Pharaoh's sword!

"Behold, God is my helper; The Lord is with those who uphold my life" (Ps. 54:4). God creates the right person and brings her to the right person.

But if you're not the right person, it doesn't matter who God brings because it won't work out. The divorce statistics on remarriage are staggering. According to Psychology Today, 50 percent of first marriages, 67 percent of second, and 73 percent of third marriages end in divorce. So, the issue isn't finding the right one; it's becoming the right one. Many marriages are in trouble because one or both of the individuals are living in a dream world about what kind of marriage is great, but marriages should be lived in reality not fantasy.

The reason marriage has been so hard isn't because your spouse is necessarily a bad person. Good people have a tough time also. Can you imagine two people from different social and cultural backgrounds coming together? Yes, but it will require work for it to succeed.

We've been asking for something that marriage can't give, which is why marriages end up in divorce. So, the quest becomes to find Mr. or Mrs. Right, thinking that will solve everything, but we've given no thought to becoming Mr. or Mrs. Right.

Here's the secret no one talks about: You can't change anyone except yourself, and you can't control anyone's actions except your own. You do your part regardless of what your spouse does; allow God to work on them because He is the only one that changes people.

You can't change your spouse by nagging; only Jesus can. Give them to Jesus and go on your knees on their behalf.

> Two are better than one because they have a good reward for their labor. For if they fall, one will lift up his companion. But woe to him who is alone when he falls, for he has no one to help him up. Again, if two lie down together, they will keep warm; but how can one be warm alone? Though one may be overpowered by another, two can withstand him. And a threefold cord is not quickly broken.
>
> —Ecclesiastes 4:9–12

The power of this passage is that it shows the benefits of marriage, some of which are supporting each other, warming each other and helping each other. That starts with being supportive, warming, and helpful, not expecting it or demanding it.

Family Is a Lifetime Glue

That's the picture of marriage God gives us. Verse 24 says, "be joined" or "cleave," which is an old King James English, and today would be like applying super glue to two glass cups. God's design is for two people to spend their lives together. We live in a world where everything is disposable, but marriage is supposed to last. That's why they were naked and not ashamed.

They were naked physically but emotionally as well. When you have a spouse that's your best friend, there's nothing you can't tell them. Here's what we realized the biggest difference was: we're Christians and we need to know that though we are in love in marriage, marriage requires work to be successful most especially in this godless society. Let me tell you, marriage is meant for life, but it requires work. Success in marriage won't happen by just wishing it, it requires prayer.

CONCLUSION

You and I live in a wicked, godless age. Unless we are grounded, we will drift in our devotion to the Lord. So, anchor yourself; the family is still relevant. Most importantly, it will help you in your eternal quest. Regardless of what storms come, you can weather them with confidence, anchored to the solid rock of Jesus Christ and His family.

Sometimes we go through difficult times in our lives. Like ships in a storm, we can be tossed around by the wind, needing help to remain stable. But the family as an anchor will never fail. He promised to build His family; I believe Him.

Self-Examination

- At the end of this book, you will know the foundation and the purpose of marriage according to God's mind.
- At the end of this book, you will know that God is not merely an observer of people's marriage but also a marriage participant.
- At the end of this book, you will know that God's marriage should be the standard of evaluation for all the marriages between men and women.
- At the end of this book, you will know some helpful secrets to a successful marriage.
- At the end of this book, you will be able to identify the keys to living a happy marital life and the ways to avoid pitfalls that leads to divorce.
- Finally, at the end of this book, you must be committed to expressing all the truth that you have acquired in God's roles in marriage.

Call to Action

So, I encourage you to stand firm in the grace given to you by your heavenly Father and say, "I will believe God's promises for me and walk in the way of His plan for my life, family, and marriage because my hope is in Christ, and only He can help me."

KEYS TO HELP YOU AVOID DIVORCE

Pragmatics/Economics

Establish Your Own Private Home

> A man shall leave his father and mother and be joined to his wife, and they shall become one flesh.
>
> —Gen. 2:24

My Conclusion: God's principle is that a married couple should move out of their parents' homes and establish their own, even if finances require something modest, such as a one-bedroom apartment. A husband and wife should decide this together, as one, and remain firm even if someone opposes. Many marriages would be improved if this principle were carefully followed.

Be Reasonable in Money Matters

> Love suffers long and is kind; love does not envy; love does not parade itself, is not puffed up; does not behave rudely, does not seek its own, is not provoked, thinks no evil.
>
> —1 Cor.13:4–5

> . . . God loves a cheerful giver.
>
> —2 Cor. 9:7

My Conclusion: Household income should be shared in a marriage, with each partner having the right to spend a certain portion as desired and according to the family budget. Separate bank accounts tend to remove the opportunity to deepen trust, which is vital for a healthy marriage. Money management is a team effort. Both should be involved, but one spouse should take ultimate responsibility. Money management roles should be determined by personal abilities and preferences.

General Advice and Tips

Continue Your Courtship

> And above all things have fervent love for one another, for 'love will cover a multitude of sins'.
>
> —1 Peter 4:8

> Her husband … praises her.
>
> —Prov. 31:28

> … But she who is married cares … how she may please her husband.
>
> —1 Cor. 7:34

> Be kindly affectionate to one another … in honor giving preference to one another.
>
> —Rom. 12:10

My Conclusion: Continue—or revive—your courtship into your married life. Successful marriages don't just happen; they must be developed. Don't take one another for granted or the resulting monotony could harm your marriage. Keep your love for one another growing by expressing it to each other; otherwise, love might fade, and you could drift apart. Love and happiness are not found by seeking them for yourself, but rather by giving them to others. So, spend as much time as possible doing things together. Learn to greet each other with enthusiasm. Relax, visit, sightsee, and eat together.

Don't overlook the little courtesies, encouragements, and affectionate acts. Surprise each other with gifts or favors. Try to "out-love" each other. Don't try to take more out of your marriage than you put into it. Lack of love is the biggest destroyer of marriage. There is also a very implausible and incoherent sequence in the social world. This sequence puts the period of courtship as a premarital thing only. Courtship which features learning and observing your partner should not end immediately the couples are pronounced married. Courtship should continue even in marriage. You should always retain that vibe that is stirred within you when you visit your spouse or spend a weekend or a holiday with your spouse during the premarital days.

Never Go to Bed Angry with One Another

> Do not let the sun go down on your wrath.
>
> —Eph. 4:26

> Confess your trespasses to one another.
>
> —James 5:16

> … Forgetting those things which are behind.
>
> —Phil. 3:13

> And be kind to one another, tenderhearted, forgiving one another, even as God in Christ forgave you.
>
> —Eph. 4:32

My Conclusion: To remain angry over hurts and grievances—big or little—can be dangerous. Unless addressed in a timely manner, even little problems can become set in your mind as convictions and can adversely affect your outlook on life. This is why God said to let your anger cool before going to bed. Be big enough to forgive and to say, "I'm sorry." After all, no one is perfect, and you are both on the same team, so be gracious enough to admit a mistake when you make it. Besides, making up is a very pleasant experience, with unusual powers to draw marriage partners closer together. God suggests it and it works!

Keep the Family Circle Tightly Closed

> You shall not commit adultery.
>
> —Ex. 20:14

> The heart of her husband safely trusts her … She does him good and not evil all the days of her life.
>
> —Prov. 31:11–12

> … The Lord has been witness between you and the wife of your youth, with whom you have dealt treacherously …
>
> —Mal. 2:14

> Keep you from the evil woman … Do not lust after her beauty in your heart, nor let her allure you with her eyelids. Can a man take fire to his bosom and his clothes not be burned? So is he who goes in to his neighbor's wife; whoever touches her shall not be innocent.
>
> —Prov. 6:24–25, 27, 29

My Conclusion: Private family matters should never be shared with others outside your home—not even parents. A person outside the marriage to sympathize with or listen to complaints can be used by the devil to estrange the hearts of a husband and wife. Solve your private home problems privately. No one else, except a minister or a marriage counselor, should be involved. Always be truthful with each other and never keep secrets. Avoid telling jokes at the expense of your spouse's feelings and vigorously defend each other. Adultery will always hurt you and everyone else in your family. God, who knows our mind, body, and feelings said, "You shall not commit adultery" (Ex. 20:14). If flirtations have already begun, break them off immediately—or shadows could settle over your life that cannot be easily lifted.

Remember that Criticism and Nagging Destroy Love

> Husbands love your wives and do not be bitter toward them.
>
> —Col. 3:19

> Better to dwell in the wilderness, than with a contentious and angry woman.
>
> —Prov. 21:19

> A continual dripping on a very rainy day and a contentious woman are alike.
>
> —Prov. 27:15

> "Why do you look at the speck in your brother's eye, but do not consider the plank in your own eye?"
>
> —Matt. 7:3

> Love suffers long and is kind; love does not envy; love does not parade itself …
>
> —1 Cor. 13:4

My Conclusion: Stop criticizing, nagging, and finding fault in your partner. Your spouse might lack much, but criticism won't help. Expecting perfection will bring bitterness to you and your spouse. Overlook faults and hunt for the good things. Don't try to reform, control, or compel your partner— you will destroy love. Only God can change people. A sense of humor, a cheerful heart, kindness, patience, and affection will banish many of your marriage problems. Try to make your spouse happy rather than good, and the good will likely take care of itself. The secret of a successful marriage lies not in having the right partner, but in being the right partner.

Do Not Overdo Anything; Be Temperate

> And everyone who competes for the prize is temperate in all things …
>
> —1 Cor. 9:25

> Love … does not seek its own.
>
> —1 Cor. 13:4–5

> Therefore, whether you eat or drink, or whatever you do, do all to the glory of God.
>
> —1 Cor. 10:31

> But I discipline my body and bring it into subjection …
>
> —1 Cor. 9:27

> Marriage is honorable among all, and the bed undefiled …
>
> —Heb. 13:4

My Conclusion: Overdoing will ruin your marriage. So will underdoing. Time with God, work, love, rest, exercise, play, meals, and social contact must be balanced in a marriage or something will snap. Too much work and a lack of rest, proper food, and exercise can lead a person to be critical, intolerant, and negative. The Bible also recommends a temperate sex life (1 Cor. 7:3–6) because degrading and intemperate sex acts can destroy love and respect for one another. Social contact with others is essential; true happiness won't be found in isolation. We must learn to laugh and enjoy wholesome, good times. To be serious all the time is dangerous. Overdoing or underdoing in anything weakens the mind, body, conscience, and the ability to love and respect one another. Don't let intemperance damage your marriage.

Respect Each Other's Personal Rights and Privacies

> Love suffers long and is kind; … Love does not envy … does not behave rudely, does not seek its own [in selfishness] … does not rejoice in iniquity … believes all things, hopes all things, and endures all things.
>
> —1 Cor. 13:4–7

> Be kindly affectionate to one another with brotherly love, in honor giving preference to one another.
>
> —Rom. 12:10

My Conclusion: Your husband or wife even has a right to be wrong part of the time and is entitled to an "off-day" without being given the third degree. Marriage partners do not own each other and should never try to force personality changes. Only God can make such changes. Confidence and trust in one another are essential for happiness, so don't check up on each other constantly. Spend less time trying to "figure out" your spouse and more time trying to please her or him. This works wonders.

Be Clean, Modest, Orderly, and Dutiful

> In like manner also, that the women adorn themselves in modest apparel.
>
> —1 Tim. 2:9

> She … willingly works with her hands. … She also rises while it is yet night and provides food for her household. … She watches over the ways of her household and does not eat the bread of idleness.
>
> —Prov. 31:13, 15, 27

> Be clean.
>
> —Is. 52:11

> Let all things be done decently and in order.
>
> —1 Cor. 14:40

> But if anyone does not provide for His own, and especially for those of His household, he has denied the faith and is worse than an unbeliever.
>
> —1 Tim. 5:8

> That you do not become sluggish …
>
> —Heb. 6:12

My Conclusion: Laziness and disorder can be used by the devil to destroy your respect and affection for one another and, thus, harm your marriage. Modest attire and clean, well-groomed bodies are important for both husband and wife. Both partners should take care to create an environment that is clean and orderly, as this will bring peace and calmness. A lazy spouse who doesn't contribute to the household is a disadvantage to the family and is displeasing to God. Anything done for one another should be done with care and respect. Carelessness in these seemingly small matters have caused division in countless homes.

Talk Things Over Freely with One Another

> Love suffers long and is kind; love does not envy; love does not parade itself, is not puffed up.
>
> —1 Cor. 13:4

> He who disdains instruction despises his own soul …
>
> —Prov. 15:32

> Do you see a man wise in his own eyes? There is more hope for a fool than for him.
>
> —Prov. 26:12

My Conclusion: Few things will strengthen your marriage more than open discussions on major decisions. Changing jobs, purchasing something expensive, and other life decisions should involve both husband and wife—differing opinions should be respected. Talking things over together will avoid many blunders that could greatly weaken your marriage. If, after much discussion and earnest prayer, opinions still differ, the wife should submit to her husband's decision, which should be motivated by his deep love for his wife and his responsibility for her well- being (see Eph. 5:22–25).

THEOLOGY AND SPIRITUALITY

Remember God is the Founder of Your Marriage

> For this reason, a man shall leave his father and mother and be joined to his wife … So then, they are no longer two but one flesh. Therefore, what God has joined together, let no man separate.
>
> —Matt. 19:5– 6

My Conclusion: Has love nearly disappeared from your home? While the devil wants to break apart your marriage by tempting you to give up, don't forget that God Himself joined you together in marriage, and He desires that you stay together and be happy. He will bring happiness and love into your lives if you will obey His divine commandments. "With God all things are possible" (Matt.19:26). Don't despair. God's Spirit can change your heart and your spouse's heart if you will ask and let Him.

The wrong kind of thinking can destroy your marriage.

Keep Christ in the Center of Your Home

> Unless the Lord builds the house, they labor in vain who build it.
>
> —Ps. 127:1

> In all your ways acknowledge Him, and He shall direct your paths.
>
> —Prov. 3:6

> And the peace of God, which surpasses all understanding, will guard your hearts and minds through Christ Jesus.
>
> —Phil. 4:7

My Conclusion: This really is the greatest principle, because it's the one that enables all the others. The vital ingredient of happiness in the home is not in diplomacy, strategy, or our effort to overcome problems, but rather in our union with Christ. Hearts filled with Christ's love will not be far apart for long. With Christ in the home, a marriage has a greater chance at being successful. Jesus can wash away bitterness and disappointment and restore love and happiness

Pray Together

> "Watch and pray, lest you enter into temptation. The spirit indeed is willing, but the flesh is weak."
>
> —Matt. 26:41

> Pray for one another.
>
> —James 5:16

> If any of you lacks wisdom, let him ask of God, who gives to all liberally …
>
> —James 1:5

My Conclusion: Pray with one another! This is a wonderful activity that will help your marriage succeed beyond your wildest dreams. Kneel before God and ask Him for true love for one another, for forgiveness, for strength, for wisdom—for the solution to problems. God will answer. By praying, you give God greater access to change your heart and actions.

Agree That Divorce is Not the Answer

> … what God has joined together, let not man separate.
>
> —Matt. 19:6

> " … Whoever divorces his wife, except for sexual immorality, and marries another, commits adultery; and whoever marries her who is divorced commits adultery."
>
> —Matt. 19:9

> The woman who has a husband is bound by the law to her husband as long as he lives …
>
> —Rom.7:2

My Conclusion: The Bible says that the ties of marriage are meant to be unbreakable. Divorce is allowed only in cases of adultery. But even then, it is not demanded. Forgiveness is always better than divorce, even in the case of unfaithfulness.

When God ordained the first marriage in Eden, He designed it for life. Thus, marriage vows are among the most solemn and binding for a person to take on. Remember, God meant for marriage to elevate our lives and meet our needs but you can only find complete fulfillment of your needs in Christ. Harboring thoughts of divorce will tend to destroy your marriage. Divorce is always destructive and is almost never a solution to the problem; instead, it usually creates greater problems— financial troubles, grieving children, etc.

God Sets the Standard for Love, So Make It Your Daily Goal to Measure Up to It

> Love suffers long and is kind; love does not envy; love does not parade itself, is not puffed up; does not behave rudely, does not seek its own, is not provoked, thinks no evil; does not rejoice in iniquity, but rejoices

> in the truth; bears all things, believes all things, hopes all things, endures all things.
>
> —1 Corinthians 13:4–7

My Conclusion: This Bible passage is one of God's greatest descriptions of love. Read it again and again. Have you made these words a part of your marriage experience? True love is not mere sentimental impulse, but rather a holy principle that involves every aspect of your married life. With true love, your marriage stands a far greater chance for success; without it, a marriage will likely fail quickly.

Morality, Character, and Discipline

Commit to Speaking Softly and Kindly

> A soft answer turns away wrath, but a harsh word stirs up anger.
>
> —Prov. 15:1

> Live joyfully with the wife whom you love …
>
> —Ecc. 9:9

> … when I became a man, I put away childish things.
>
> —1 Cor. 13:11

My Conclusion: Always speak softly and kindly to your spouse—even in disputes. Decisions made when angry, tired, or discouraged are unreliable anyway, so it's best to relax and let anger cool before speaking. And when you do speak, let it always be quietly and lovingly. Harsh, angry words can crush your spouse's desire to hear and please you.

APPENDIX

Thoughts and Questions

1. Which marriage partner should be the first to make peace after a quarrel?

> The one who was in the right!

2. Is there a principle for in-laws interfering in our family decisions?

> Yes! Do not interfere with your son's or daughter's marriage unless your counsel is requested by both partners (see 1 Thess. 4:11.) Many marriages that might have been a little heaven on earth have been damaged by in-laws. The duty of all in-laws is to leave the decisions made in the newly-established home strictly alone.

3. My spouse is godless, and I am trying to be a Christian. His influence is terrible. Should I divorce him?

> No! Read 1 Corinthians 7:12–14 and 1 Peter 3:1– 2. God wants you to dwell with him if he is willing to stay in the marriage because you may be used to win him to Christ.

4. My spouse ran off with another person. Now repentant, she wants to return home. My pastor says I should take her back, but God forbids this, doesn't He?

> No, indeed! God permits divorce for adultery, yes, but He does not command it. Forgiveness is always better

and is always preferred. (See Matt. 6:14–15.) Divorce will seriously mar your life and the lives of your children. Give her another chance! The golden rule (Matt. 7:12) applies here. If you and your wife will turn your lives over to Christ, He will make your marriage supremely happy. It is not too late.

5. What can I do? Men are always coming on to me.

Some men refuse to control their impulses, however, as a woman, a few things you might do to help ward off unwanted attention is to dress modestly, avoid suggestive conversation or flirting, or engaging in activities that invite attention. There is something about Christian ethics and dignity that keeps a man in His place. Christ said, "Let your light so shine before men, that they may see your good works and glorify your Father in heaven" (Matt. 5:16).

6. Can you tell me plainly what God's counsel is to one who has fallen but is repentant?

Long ago Christ gave a pointed and comforting answer to one who had fallen into immorality but was repentant. "… Jesus … said to her, 'Woman, where are those accusers of yours? Has no one condemned you?' She said, 'No one, Lord.' And Jesus said to her, 'Neither do I condemn you; go and sin no more'" (John 8:10–11). His forgiveness and counsel still apply today.

7. Isn't the "innocent party" in a divorce sometimes partially guilty also?

Certainly. Sometimes the innocent party, by a lack of love, inattentiveness, self-righteousness, unkindness, selfishness, nagging, or downright coldness, can encourage evil thoughts and actions in his or her spouse. Sometimes the "innocent party" might be as guilty before God as the "guilty" one. God looks upon our motives, seeing past our actions. "... for the Lord does not see as man sees; for man looks at the outward appearance, but the Lord looks at the heart" (1 Sam. 16:7).

8. Does God expect me to live with a physically abusive spouse?

Physical abuse can be life-threatening and is a serious problem that demands immediate attention. The spouse and family members who have been physically abused must find a safe environment in which to live. Both husband and wife need to seek the help of God and professional help through a qualified Christian marriage counsellor—and in some cases separation is often appropriate.

The Reality of Marriage

Some people believe that marriage is the solution to all their problems; that marriage involves sitting on a beach in the moonlight, holding hands at the movies, and seeing their beloved as the most beautiful and immaculate being in the world.

But when couples marry, other important concerns such as bills, mortgage, and dirty diapers enter the equation and suddenly romance flies out of the window.

In fact, in a short amount of time, those little idiosyncrasies that you found so appealing about your spouse have turned into irritants. What's more, your partner may expect you to look after the kids, keep the house neat, cook sumptuous meals, be great in bed and even make some money. You may think you can't do all that at once, and you're right.

You expect your spouse to lend a helping hand in the kitchen, and at least once in a while, volunteer to look after the children. Naturally, according to you, your spouse should automatically remember your birthday and your wedding anniversary, refrain from leaving dirty clothes around, and take you out for dinner once in a while and bring flowers home after work—but most often it doesn't work out this way, does it?

The Importance of Friendship

Marriage requires constant effort. A good marriage is built on the unshakeable foundation of compromise, compassion, and loyalty. It demands that you're true to the vows you took together.

Friendship is important. If you're friends when you get married, you can remain friends. Good friends support each other and help each other grow spiritually and creatively. Growth requires both gentleness and firmness, even firmness at times, but the ultimate motive must be to help each other grow.

Some Tips to Keep Your Marriage Fresh

I hope these points will not be repetitive, but important, which is why I am re-emphasizing it.

So, ask yourself whether you really know each other. Or have you confused sexual compatibility with "happily ever after"?

Try these positive actions to get to know each other better and still keep your marriage fresh:

- If the zing has gone out of your sex life, reignite it. Do something new together in bed.
- Pay attention to your appearance. Refrain from showing your partner a sloppy version of yourself, dressed in a worn-out outfit, not showered, with your hair unkempt. No matter how familiar you are with each other, you can still be the sex symbol you used to be before you got married.
- Go on a vacation together, just the two of you. Travel to a romantic getaway and allow the sunrise to breathe more warmth into your relationship. Run barefoot on

the beach. Indulge each other with your kind of sensual massage.

- Open up and talk to each other about your challenges without losing your temper. Talking about these issues is extremely important, but try doing it in a peaceful, beautiful setting when you're both relaxed.
- Do the things you used to enjoy doing together in the beginning of your relationship. Remember the personality traits that initially attracted you to your spouse. It might be that these qualities are still attractive, but it's you who has changed.

In every marriage more than a week old, there are grounds for divorce. The trick is to find, and continue to find, grounds for marriage.

—Robert Anderson

Marriage Counseling

You could try Christian marriage counseling if you're having great difficulty solving your challenges by yourselves. Most marriage counselors say that ailing relationships have some factors in common. These are:

- Money issues
- Sex
- Time management
- Raising kids
- The strain that may come from extended family
- Ineffective communication
- Trust issues

The trick is to know exactly where the root of your situation lies. It could even be a combination of these.

However, if drug and alcohol abuse or physical and emotional violence are involved, your marriage definitely needs help. Until these grave abusive issues are resolved, you should find a place to go where you and your children can be safe, away from your spouse.

STUDY GUIDE

General Introduction

Marriage is one of the most powerful institutions in life. In it, there is life and death, sorrow and joy, fulfillment and failure, regression and progression, conflict and unity, and much more. Those who are in this institution still search for answers to some of the fundamental questions posed therein. On the other hand, those who are yet to be in this institution are curious and bothered about what such a vital institution of life has in stock for them. However, whether you are married or yet to marry, the specific marital contents that you desire are entirely dependent on having the right insights and being a practical example of those insights. If you want to have a fulfilled, joyful, enlivened, progressive, and peaceful marriage, you should seek guidance directly from the word of God. In this study guide, you will be imparted through divinely inspired answers to the fundamental questions of marriage. You will have access to the ancient wisdom of God concerning marriage.

For clear understanding, this study guide has been sectionalized.

At the completion of each section, you will be asked some questions and provided scriptures to guide you into making decisions that are inspired by God. In some cases, there are answers already provided to these questions. The purpose of the answers is to guide you into answering the question your own way. In some cases, you are required to study the scriptures individually and provide answers by yourself.

Food for Thought

- What benefits does the word of God hold for me in my marital decisions?
- Psalm 1:1–3, Psalm 119:105, 2 Timothy 3:16–17, Proverbs 3:5–6, Jeremiah 29:11.

- With God, can a dead marriage come to life again? Ezekiel 37:3–6, Hosea 6:2.

Prayer Point

I thank you God for you have shown interest in guiding me in my marriage and marital decisions. As I give myself wholly to your wisdom concerning the issue of marriage, I pray that you grant me quick understanding on all you have to teach me. Amen.

Week 1: Chapter 1

Summary

- In this chapter, it was taught that Jesus Christ is God (John 1:1, Heb.1:3, Is. 9:6).
- In this chapter, you were taught that marriage was first originated and participated by the God, Jesus Christ and His church (Gen. 2:24, Eph. 5:31–32).
- In this chapter, you were taught that the church is a body of believing human beings. (1 Corinthians 12:27)
- In this chapter, you were taught to emulate the roles of God in His marriage and you were introduced to the contractual terms of God's marriage with the church, the body of humans that believed Him (Jer. 31:34, Eph. 1:3, Hosea 2:19–21, Eph. 5:21–22).
- In this chapter, you were taught that it takes God Himself to work in you for you to be able to emulate the roles of God in His marriage (Phil. 2:3, 1 Cor. 2:14).

Questions

What is the difference between God's marriage and man's marriage?

The contract of God's marriage is eternal. Its benefits and its terms have no end (Hosea 2:19–21, Rev. 19:6–9).

Do I have the power to perform the roles of God in my marriage?

Every believer has the power to do the will of God on earth as it is done in heaven (Matt. 6:9–10, 1 John 4:17).

According to this chapter, out of truth and perception which should you uphold in marriage?

In Jesus' era, the people's perception was that the temple of God was the physical church. However, according to the truth of God's word, Jesus upheld Himself as the temple of God (John 2:18–22). In the same light, the people in your world may have the wrong perception about your spouse as unworthy, unfitting, ugly, or poor. You may even have a physical perception that your spouse is no longer beautiful or handsome, or that your spouse now has excessive fats in their body. However, you are to uphold the truth of God's word over this negative perception. Present your spouse to yourself as spotless, perfect, and blameless before you (Eph. 5:27).

Week 2: Chapter 2

Summary

- In this chapter, there was a reorientation on some of the misconceptions about the gospel.

- In this chapter, you were given the wedding invitation to the eternal marriage of Jesus Christ (1 Cor. 15:1–4, Rev.19:6–9).

Questions

What does the Bride (the church) of Jesus Christ stand to gain in God's marriage?

> There is no measure to the abundance of blessings that the bride of Jesus Christ stands to gain. Imagine yourself to be greatly blessed by the creator of heaven and earth. According to the book of Revelation, God always speaks about the blessing of those who agree to honor His wedding invitation to His Son (Rev. 19:9).

According to this chapter, what is the implication of having the wrong invitation letter at the feast of God's eternal marriage? (Matt. 22:1–14).

Week 3: Chapter 3

Summary

- In this chapter, you were taught the need to diligently guard your hearts to have a fulfilled marital life (Prov. 4:20-23).
- In this chapter, you were shown twelve attitudinal detriments that can destroy your marriage (Col. 3:9, Prov. 14:7).

Questions

What if one's father or mother gives one bad counsel in marriage ("Divorce him! Do not cook for him! Your wife is like your slave, don't give her freedom!") is one still obligated to follow their counsel since God said, "Honor your father and mother"?

> There is a spirit in man and the inspiration of the Almighty gives them understanding (Job 32:8). Once you have a genuine understanding that the counsel your parents provide you in your marriage is against that of God, you are at liberty to reject such counsel without disregarding. A perfect example of that was Jonathan who humbly rejected the counsel of Saul his father concerning the murder of innocent David (1 Sam. 19:1–5).

Week 4: Chapter 4

Summary

- In this chapter, you were taught the power and characteristics of God's Word.
- In this chapter, you were taught that the Word of God is Jesus Christ, and He is inseparable from God.
- In this chapter, you were taught that a negative use of your word has a great destructive power.

Questions

Having understood that partners in marriage have been unified to be one, if one of the partners uses words negatively in the marriage and the other one uses words positively, which of the words will prevail?

> Let us first appeal to our natural observation. If there are two people in a room and one of these two people brings darkness and the other bring light, surely the light will overcome the darkness. In cases where the

two people bring light, the room will be brighter than it was. In the same way, if your partner has a negative perception of your marriage, you are to keep revealing God's perception and word until it has prevalence over the negative one (John 1:5). With God-inspired words, you will create a godly marital home.

Week 5: Chapter 5

Summary

- In this chapter, you were taught that your enemy the devil, not human beings (Eph. 6:11–12).
- In this chapter, you were taught some of the defining characteristics of the devil (John 13:2, 1 Thess. 2:18, Rev. 12:9, John 8:44).
- In this chapter, you were taught some of the devices the devil adopts to destroy marriages. (2 Cor. 2:11–12).

Questions

How can one conquer the devil in one's marriage?

Truth: Let truth be the foundation of all things.

Righteousness: Order your conducts according to the will of God.

Peace: Let the gospel of peace always be your source of inspiration.

Faith: Have faith in all the promises of God for a godly marriage.

The Word of God: Constantly refresh your mind and heart with the study of the word of God.

Prayer: Pray to God always (Eph. 6:10–18).

What if the devil has completely ruined my marriage and we have reached the level of divorce, can I start a new marriage with a new spouse?

> The scripture condemns you to remarry. So far, your ex-spouse is still alive, you can only remain single or rejoined to your ex-spouse. However, you can put the power of resurrection into work by raising your dead marriage back to life. Remember that your enemy is not your husband or wife but the devil. You can initiate reconciliation as you wage war on the devil (1 Cor. 7:10–11, 27).

Week 6: Chapter 6

Summary

- In this chapter, you were taught the common problems in marriage.

Questions

- Is it wrong for you to abstain from sex through fasting and prayer for twenty-one days even though your partner doesn't consent to it? (1 Cor. 7:4–5).
- In your own view, what are the marital consequences of the problems highlighted in this chapter?
- Clearly present ten ways you would like to celebrate your marriage.

Week 7: Chapter 7

Summary

- In the study, you were taught a good family must be built upon a marital foundation in the same way a good marriage must be built upon the foundation of Jesus Christ.
- In the study, you were taught that marital values should ultimately be drawn from the Word of God and not from the degrading laws and practices of the society.
- In the study, more emphasis was laid on the significant truth that Christ is the purpose of all marriage or family. It must showcase Christ to the world through love.
- In the study, you were taught that building a family with an incomplete individual such as an unbeliever is destructive to family.
- In the study, you were taught that the culture of divorce is an alien culture in the kingdom of God.

Questions

- What if the bed has been defiled, can a Christian still build a godly marriage and family? (Ps. 89:30–35, Heb. 9:12, Ez. 36:33).
- Having learnt that the man is the head of the family, can the woman assume leadership position in cases where the man has clearly failed? (1 Sam. 25:1–35).
- What happens when the father fails in his parental duties on the children? (1 Sam. 1:22–34).

Week 8: Chapter 8

Summary

- In the study, you were exposed to some keys that could help marriages avoid divorce.

Questions

What if one spouse defiled their marriage vow, can a Christian survive or be revived?

> Yes, if both are willing. Take your marriage up to God in prayer and pray for healing and that God should bring reconciliation and restore your love. Pray and "pray without ceasing" (1 Thess. 5:17).

How do I deal with anger in the marriage?

> Make sure you de-escalate any tension. Also make sure you communicate effectively. Practice patience and compassion. In addition, reflect on your actions and make sure you understand your triggers.

ABOUT THE AUTHOR

Dr. Olu Oluwa-Tofehinti is the founder of "Changing A Generation" and also the senior pastor at House of Praise Foursquare Church. He has mentored and coached many in the last twenty years. Since 2000, he's helped many transform their lives and marriages. His years of experience have taught him to always make success in life, marriage or relationship his priority.

Olu has spoken at many conferences over the years including the Foursquare Church conferences. He led many workshops during these conferences. He has also spoken in many churches in Africa, England, Ireland, and the USA. In addition, Olu has his own show on The Now Network cable network. He has been a guest on a local radio shows over the years. He was also featured in Yahoo Finance recently as one of the top ten mentors to follow in 2020.

Olu offers a wide range of speaking and coaching services with the necessary tools and expertise to help transform lives and marriages into success. He works with clients from start to finish, focusing on their needs while producing new ideas, developing effective strategies and designing high quality, customizable, and scalable solutions, inspiring couples to think and rethink with a fresh, entertaining approach. He's proud to help shape and improve many relationships. His Spirit-based approach makes him unique.

Since 1993, Dr. Olu has been helping people realize their purpose in a dynamic way. His twenty-five years of ministry and coaching experience comes in handy in his work. His delivery is exceptional, and the effect is transformational. From Africa, Europe, to North America, many people have been touched by his message of transformation, healing and love through his stewardship ministries.

He is a graduate of International Bible Institute of London, UK, the University of Greenwich, London, UK and Surrey University, UK. Olu went on to receive his doctor of divinity in 2017. Olu is an ordained minister of the International Church of the Foursquare Gospel. He has been married for thirty years with three children.

My Program

Wait! Do you want to be successful and happy in your relationships?

Since you have read my book, let me introduce you to my step-by-step exclusive program: "Secrets to Transforming Your Relationship and Avoiding Divorce."

This is a step-by-step program that will coach and guide you to reinvent yourself so you can live a happier, fulfilling marriage or relationship that you love!

Sign up at the link below:

https://www.drhollu.com/masterclass

Other Books by the Author

The Power of Personal Transformation: Steps to Living a Transformed Life. Copyright 2018, Dr. Olu Oluwa-Tofehinti.

Unshackled: The Secrets of Ruling Your World! Copyright 2018, Dr. Olu Oluwa-Tofehinti.

CPSIA information can be obtained
at www.ICGtesting.com
Printed in the USA
JSHW050328300622
27484JS00005B/43

9 781637 690482